THE MASK OF REALITY

An Approach to Design for Theatre

by

IRENE COREY

anchorage press PLAYS, inc.
PO Box 2901 Louisville KY 40201
Phone and Fax: (502) 583-2288
applays@bellsouth.net
www.applays.com

THE MASK OF REALITY: An Approach to Design for Theatre
Copyright, 1968, by The Anchorage Press
All rights reserved.
First Printing, 1968
Second Printing, 1976
Third Printing, 1988
ISBN 0-87602-007-4

Printed and bound in Singapore
by Singapore National Printers Ltd through Palace Press

Dedication

If this were my book alone I would dedicate it to my husband, Orlin Corey; but it is the record of our mutual work in the theatre and is already inseparably a part of him.

So together we offer it as a tribute to those young people who worked with us; who, having caught the vision of our concepts, lent them a bit of their life.

IRENE COREY

Foreword

For sixteen years my husband and I have worked in educational theatre. This book is a reflection of some of the things we have learned. During this time we produced dozens of plays of all types, including those which seek to show natural man in his society as it appears. Yet, beneath the world of appearance is a true world of reality, and it was our combined search in this direction which led us to the most rewarding results.

There are many books on design for the conventional theatre of appearance; this book attempts to look beneath the exterior to find a "mask" for the underlying reality.

IRENE COREY

Contents

Introduction

It has long been popular to think of art as "pure" and of the artist as one who dwells in the realm of idea, never compromising his imagination with "technique" or soiling his hand with matter. Admittedly, unless all is accident, idea must come first; but is it accurate to rate, as tests now do, those who can claim the greatest number and variety of ideas as having the most "creativity"? At a recent seminar on that elusive term, a lawyer remarked, "I may have a thousand ideas, none of which works, while another man may have only one, and it may work so well that we rightly call him a genius." The chances are that if the one idea works it is through modification in the working, through the development and execution of subsequent ideas arrived at in process.

The artist, that is, must have skill and must deal in matter. The hand and the material at hand are as much forming elements as the mind —perhaps more, since whatever gets onto paper or canvas or the stage *exists*, regardless of its merit and regardless of its failure to duplicate the original concept. The piece of sculpture is not the image in the sculptor's mind, but whatever the stone is cut to.

The Christian story of creation and redemption may serve as an example of the working of the "artist" in idea and matter. God had the idea of man and molded him out of clay. But the matter made its own demands: woman had to be formed too, and she in turn demanded knowledge, which brought sin and death into the world. But — although He came near erasing the whole affair with forty days of rain — God kept working until, *using* woman and sin and death, He brought the story full round to redemption. Even God had to "grope it out" (Robert Frost's phrase) according to the bias of the material.

So it is that this book, which is an "invitation to imagination," speaks in terms of existing, often limiting, conditions — the given play, the director's concept, the actor, the stage, human and animal traits, colors and forms, muslin and paper and glue. An imagination unlimited spins aimlessly in a vacuum; with no obstacle to overcome, it finds no place to get a foothold. The imagination must be disciplined to the conditions of form and circumstance and matter.

Irene Corey thinks with her hands and her scissors as well as with her mind — but always with consummate discipline. She invites her readers to do the same. Though we may — and must — learn from others, each must work with the given material himself, shaping it to his own concept with his own hand. Imitation, Emerson has said, is suicide. Irene Corey presents her work here not to be copied, but to encourage our own disciplined effort to bring the reality we perceive to artistic reality in the theatre.

"Corey theatre" is demanding theatre. I have been associated with it for more than a decade as actor, playwright, and audience. It consistently demands of me my hardest work, my most unremitting self-criticism, my best attention — and it gives me a sense of achievement seldom come by. I trust that this attempt to get onto paper what exists essentially in time, space, and motion will make equal demands upon the reader.

Robert Canzoneri
Worthington, Ohio

1

To Enhance the Theatre

"What is there common to all forms embodying an aspect of the inapprehensible? It is their revelation of the presence of an Other World, not necessarily infernal or celestial . . . rather a supra real world existing here and now. For all alike . . . this 'real' is mere appearance and something else exists, that is not appearance."

André Malraux
The Metamorphosis of the Gods

PRIMITIVE MASKS have been a source of curiosity, inspiration and wonder since their discovery by contemporary man. What gives them their sense of acute vitality? What spirit pervades them that refuses to die, even before the skeptical gaze of an analytical, scientific intellect? Behind these intriguing animal-man-spirit images, so charged with inner meaning, is there a secret which may guide us toward effective theatrical design? Is there any difference between the mysteries evoked on an earthen circle "stage," vibrating to the rhythm of a tribal dance, and those celebrated on the boards of a thrust stage surrounded by a twentieth century audience?

What aspects of experience do we today have such difficulty understanding? Those which are intangible, which defy being bought, held in the hand, put in the bank, locked in a drawer; the tender and terrifying interrelationships of ourselves with other people; the gossamer threads of tension or grace existing between us. How do we comprehend love? What is the nature of the power of hate? What is the corrosive destruction released by greed? If we founder in understanding the abstractions of our relation to other people, how much more difficult it is to establish our relation to God.

Throughout the entire primitive world existed the belief in a universal energy which pervades all things. Today we have seen that life force as a chain reaction. William Fagg and Margaret Plass present the theory that in primitive art a common manifestation of this life force is expressed through repeated use of the exponential curve, as seen in a neck, a back, or a horn.

I submit that we of the theatre seek to find symbols and shapes to capture, and to control the same life force which permeated the primitive world.

1

The primitive sculptor had an advantage over us in that he did not separate reality and unreality. The supernatural and the natural together wove the fabric of his daily life. The artist served his community by integrating the world of the real with the unreal by the use of symbols which, growing out of commonly shared experiences and concepts, had meaning for his neighbors. But we, self-proclaimed realists for these many centuries, have accepted materialism—matter alone—as ample reason for living. Within the framework of our commercial climate, the art and theatre we produce evokes in its merely physical implications no wonder, and little excitement. Eventually our dissatisfaction must lead us into a search for the lost abstractions.

I am not concerned with a theatre of diversion. The great plays lift invisible relationships of men into forms which can be seen and examined. The visualization of abstract relationships is the proper concern of the theatre artist.

In primitive societies the artist did not speak as an individual. As a funnel for all the pressures of his society, he increased the life force available to the tribe, the community, and the individual. Out of group desires and fears he shaped into physical form the symbols of gratification and security. Personal whim did not enter in. His art is "an endless incantation given visual form."

The theatrical designer operates in much the same way. He is not free to express his individual likes and dislikes. He is governed by the playwright who sets forth the entire framework, and by the director who sets forth the desired goal. The artist serves as the filter for all visual decisions. If the play requires a setting in a gingerbread Victorian house, it matters not that the designer dislikes such architecture. Does it serve the playwright's intention? What selected details from such architecture best express the mood of the play, the character of the inhabitants? What overall shape will best accommodate a visualization of the directorial approach? All of the contributing factors — architecture, characterization, mood, costume, period, social structure, and philosophic thought — are like the fragments of glass in a kaleidoscope. The artist becomes the cylinder which organizes them into significant visual design.

It is not enough that the devices chosen have meaning only for the designer. The artist should serve as a seer, grappling with elements of the community, and directing the forces he has channeled to the community. There is no ivory tower, no inward attic for the theatre. A play is created to exist in the limited space and brief time when it is enacted before an audience. It is true that when a play is read as literature the reader becomes both actor and audience, with the mind for a stage. But this is indeed not the occasion which we call theatre, and this is not the purpose for which the dialogue is written. Drama is the art of implication by use of word, gesture, intonation, and atmosphere. Consciously or subconsciously, designed images must communicate.

The primitive artist used humanity as a mere point of departure, giving shape and form to those abstract life forces surrounding him. Realistic details were submerged in the greater task of capturing the spirit of this other life. Of course, the theatrical designer can, by thoughtful selection of realistic details, automatically relate to the viewers valid information about the play. In any work

Sketch for Setting of "Hedda Gabler."

of art, however, the external attributes are only a means to an end. The underlying idea, philosophy, or *life force* will be of an abstract nature. This fact indicates the designer's greatest challenge: he must give visual form to abstract ideas. Only when the artist struggles toward this concept will the highest aspirations of the playwright and the director be approached.

How can abstractions be grasped and visualized in the theatre? It is first necessary that the designer arrive at the state of oneness with the world-of-the-play which was automatic to the primitive artist in his surroundings. There is no recipe, of course, but it is safe to advise as a beginning a long state of marination. The artist must steep himself in the script, soak up its moods, taste and analyze its overtones, undercurrents, and all the other ingredients which contribute to its unique flavor. Shadowy ideas must be pursued in the hope that their chance appearance may reveal a nuance of meaning that will enrich the texture. A free association of related ideas must be encouraged. Once immersed in the body of the play, the mind should be free to experiment, relying on the desired atmosphere of the play to determine the suitability of ideas.

The taste of the artist comes into action in the choice of the most telling shape, the most appropriate color. One of the truly stunning achievements of Cecil Beaton in *My Fair Lady* was the Ascot, called for without description, by the play. Although his research told him that people had, upon the death of King Edward VII, attended the annual race in the garb of mourning, the historical fact of the "Black Ascot" would not alone have justified his decision to use black and white for the musical scene. But since it helped to underline the artificial posing of the aristocracy and revealed a stress on fashion which upstaged even the horses, the choice was appropriate and effective. How ridiculous to assume that black and white was his favorite combination or that, if it were, he would for that reason impose it on the play!

Even traditionally staged "period" plays deserve to have their underlying abstractions probed and presented visually. Why must Hedda Gabler be bric-a-bracked into a heavy, stuffy house, with every wall papered and every sofa antimacassared? A contemporary Norwegian director says: "We will await the Ibsen producer who will tackle his problem with audacity, untrammelled by convention, purely from the standpoint of our own generation . . . showing independence and originality." The important element to be revealed is how Hedda *feels* about the house. To her it is cage, erected by her father, her husband and the pressures of society. Conceived as Hedda's prison, the walls may become scrimmed bars through which the world watches her and in which she feels the object of ridicule. Or, why use walls at all? Perhaps the room could be outlined only by an oppressive ceiling piece with the portrait of her father looming in magnified significance. The fact that Ibsen was writing for a realistic theatre does not invalidate a fresh expression of what he was saying.

Plays which were contemporary when written become "period" by the displacement of time. Incidental furnishings and fashions which were meant as mere indications of environment, jump at us because of unfamiliarity. If these elements are not organic to the play's impact, they can clutter rather than clarify. Today's *Mary, Mary* is tomorrow's grandmother.

3
Set design for *The Prisoner* by Bridgette Boland. It expresses the horror of a sinister, highly organized apparatus set against the integrity of one man's mind.

Bridget Boland's *The Prisoner* is a study of how the strongest mind can become warped, entangled and confused by persistent destructive effort. When my husband and I produced this play, we found it was not enough to confine the Cardinal in a merely physical prison. We created a maze-prison of the mind. All entrances to the cell were made from far upstage, between overlapping transparent walls which jutted alternately from stage left and stage right. Guards, officials, and the Cardinal himself wound through this grim labyrinth. Oblique diagonals repeated the strong tensions set up between the Cardinal and the prosecutor.

Although all plays can be strengthened by deep analysis, the great ones which have many sub-structures of meaning will yield possibilities for richer visualization. From these probings into the spirit of the play, forms *sometimes* appear which totally submerge the human face and body. When, in such a play, the person of the actor is completely masked, he assumes a new force which is greater than his own individuality. Richard Southern in *The Seven Ages of Theatre* states that "The magic of the mask and of its delicate substitute make-up remains as a mystery in our theatre to this day. . . Take now an 'extension' of the mask, and with it let the hands be gloved, the feet shod, the arms and legs clad, and the body invested, and you have a complete concealment of the world and a complete revelation of the supernatural." The image thus created assumes its own life-force. The actor, cloaked in non-human identity, freed of individual inhibitions, can move into a new realm of relationship with the audience: that of a super-human, mystical power.

The actor now acquires an additional set of restrictions, not his own. These serve to enlarge and stylize his power, rather than diminish it. For centuries the Noh actor has worked with his own personality completely submerged in mask and costume. In front of a mirror, he absorbs the nature of the character he is to play, seeking from the reflected image inner significance. The Kabuki actor, substituting make-up for mask, has followed the same course. Just as the boned line of a period costume or the addition of a hump or a paunch will aid in the delineation of character, so the artistic image imposes a potential for greater strength.

Gordon Craig argued that the actor is most expressive when he sacrifices literal gesture and attitude. Patterned after the actions of dolls, the movement of Kabuki is specific, sharp, and clear. It eschews the literal gesture for one that is at once stylized and of supranormal significance. It is movement taken from actuality and submitted to a rhythmical pattern.

The poet condenses a large idea to a few lines and this increases its power. The artist refines a natural object to its most important aesthetic elements to produce effective design. An actor reduces the monotonous daily actions of man into those movements which reveal character. In all cases when literal content is submerged, allowing only highly selected details to form the visible top of the iceberg of meaning, a much greater potential is suggested.

The Everyman Players' production of *The Book of Job* as seen at Pine Mountain State Park, Pineville, Kentucky. Presented in a natural amphitheatre on a geometric stage, backed by an eighty foot cliff, the mosaic figures are mirrored in a reflection pool.

5
Three of *The Book of Job* players before the Graham Sutherland tapestry in Coventry Cathedral.

My first experience with this phenomenon occured on an October evening at Georgetown College, Georgetown, Kentucky, some years ago. My husband and I had conceived the idea of presenting an arrangement of *The Book of Job* with the characters costumed and made up like Byzantine mosaic figures. We had created the jewel-toned costumes from squares of satin, and the wigs and beards from organdy. We had watched the actors painstakingly follow the make-up charts, painting onto their faces with liquid make-up each tessera. But all the elements had not coalesced until that evening. When those mosaic statues walked onto the stage, we, their creators, gasped. Gone were Pat, Don, Sandra, Bill, Joe, Charlie, and all those other young actors we knew so well. Who were these larger-than-life creatures looming before us? A persistent doubt nagged at us: "Have we gone too far?"

Since that October evening, this play has made two off-Broadway runs, has been seen at two World's Fairs, has toured the eastern United States twice, wintered in Florida, journeyed to England three times, and to South Africa for three months. Pygmalion-like, these ten figures continue to roam the earth from the play's annual summer base in Kentucky. Is it possible for such a design concept to be too large? It may have overwhelmed us, but *it was not too large for the literature it grew out of.*

6

Romans by St. Paul as presented at Southwark Cathedral, London, England. 7

Once such a strong design statement had been made, it created its own demands. In another of our productions, *Romans by Saint Paul*, the figures were patterned after the statuary adorning the portals of Gothic cathedrals. The warmth and humanity of the Apostle were designed to be correlated with his authority as a saint of the early church. A chorus of saints responded to his questions. In studying the late Gothic sculpture, we had observed that on some cathedrals the figures appear in casual attitudes of conversation, leaning out of their niches to speak with one another. This seemed a logical model for the director to use. But when he instructed the actors to assume these informal gestures, the style of their presence resisted. They had acquired such spiritual significance that even the space around them was surcharged. Sculptural fashions may have become humanized by late Gothic artists, but one cannot push a saint around.

1 2 3

Costume designs for Mrs. Stephen Douglas as seen in Norman Corwin's play, *The Rivalry*. Designed in the manner of fashion plates found in Godey's *Lady's Book*, they illustrate the principle of color progression.

Emotional response to color is potentially a powerful tool in the hands of the theatre artist. A simple example exists in Norman Corwin's *The Rivalry*. I used color progression in the costumes of Mrs. Stephen Douglas to accent the moods of the play. Responding to notes of optimism at the

9

beginning of the play, her dress was bright and light. As the tenor of the debates began to reflect the serious mood of the nation, the tensions over slavery, and the ensuing internal conflict, her dresses became more subdued, ending in widow's black as she paid homage to the dead Lincoln and Douglas.

Costume and mask design for Chorus representing time in Shakespeare's
The Winter's Tale.

Although Arthur Miller's *The Crucible* is essentially a black and gray play, I felt that the hysteria of the girls could be best expressed in color. Their drab dresses were trimmed in red, with Abigail having the strongest accent. This color emphasis was climaxed by the entrance of the hanging judges in scarlet robes. My decision could, with theatrical justification, have been based on artistic license. However, history is often a dramatic designer, too. At that period the Massachusetts Colony followed the English tradition of scarlet judicial robes.

Another abstract quality is encountered in Shakespeare's *The Winter's Tale*, where time is used as a cleansing ingredient, washing away the events of fifteen years in one sweep. In our production time became the dominant theme. The Chorus of Time, carrying a large, internally illuminated hour-glass, was introduced in the prologue and appeared in mime between all acts, symbolizing the passing years. Stage settings were composed of filmy silk hangings which were released to flow to the floor at the end of scenes. When Leontes with maniacal fury denounced his queen, the effect was as though his consuming anger had dissolved the world, which silently shuddered and disappeared at his feet.

The search of the theatrical artist for the abstract will lead him to many fields. What richer vein can be found than that of art history, which is a tangible record of man's struggle to find a way to express new ideas, to contain the life force in stone, wood, paint, and glass? Consider the power of Christianity imaged in writhing stone figures, ecstatic in conviction, or glowing with faith in heaven-bent windows. Contrast with this, images with the serene self-contentment of a Buddhist statue. Look at Michelangelo's *David*, pulsating with energy and force, a refined statement of the potential capabilities of man. Consider how

12
The hanging judges confronting John Proctor in *The Crucible*, by Arthur Miller.

13
Leontes in mourning at the opening of Act 5, *The Winter's Tale*.

the Cubists shattered their tradition bound world in order to see all sides at one time. Not content with outward appearances, they searched for the inner structure. Cannot such concepts and forms be studied and restated in theatrical terms? Is it not conceivable that a similar life force may be found flowing through the veins of a play, and that a wedding of the two may produce a new creature?

Perhaps the most lasting impression of a play is its atmosphere. Here again are more abstractions. We respond to mood, to mystery, to the magic of the unknown. It is born in us. Curiosity is roused, expectations are raised when even a simple gift is concealed with paper and a bow. We must wrap the intentions of a play in such a magical way that the audience will ache on the edge of anticipation to untie the meaning. Playing on man's response to the bright and the dark, we wrap our ideas in shadows and reveal them with light.

Play in hand, imagination in head, courage in heart, we must leave our foolish "reality" behind and meet the angels half-way.

Setting with silk hangings for the Sicilian Court, Act 1, *The Winter's Tale*.
14

2
To Design A Play

"There is no formula for inspiration. . . . (The theatre) deals not with logic but with magic."

Robert Edmund Jones
The Dramatic Imagination

THE creative process may work differently for each designer, but one must always begin with the play. This is the fountainhead of ideas for the entire production. Only after the play has been thoroughly assimilated can an approach to design be started. Design is not an alien element tacked on from the outset ("Oh, let's do a play in pink and purple!"). It must be generated from seeds planted within the play by the playwright. The resulting bloom will not always be the same for every designer, but the life force of the flowers comes from the same seedbed.

One or more dominant ideas lie within every play and there may be sub-themes branching off from the main root. All variations must be examined to determine which will receive major stress in the production. The primary accent should be decided by the director, or, if it comes from the designer's research, must be agreed upon by the director. For it is absolutely essential that director and designer travel the same road, heading for the same goal.

The result of divergent views between designer and director was seen in the 1955 production of *King Lear* at Stratford-upon-Avon, England. Costumes and settings were designed by Isamu Noguchi, the brilliant Japanese-American. The forms were reduced to stark geometrics, stunning in their simplicity. But when these highly refined designs were juxtaposed with traditional directorial approaches and realistic acting styles, both looked out of place.

The relation of the directorial concept to the visual realization is the most critical aspect of any production. What is the ideal relationship between the director and designer? I am happily married to my director, and this answers the question for me. Granting that this is not a workable solution in most situations, it may still be valid to ask why our artistic relationship works.

b, in *The Book of Job.*

A good marriage, for example, is based on mutual respect. Out of this respect grows decisions which are satisfactory to both parties. A good stage production demands a similar understanding between director and designer, with a free exchange of ideas flowing toward artistic solutions. The designer's research can serve to enrich the director's thinking even as his research may stimulate the designer's imagination, but final authority must lie with the director. An ideal state has been reached when after a production is launched, neither can remember who thought of what.

The directorial concept determines the dominant theme of the play and decides the spirit of the production. This concept will define limitations for the designer. It indicates the place, the time, and the mood, shaping the area of research.

The Book of Job dramatization will serve as an example of the design procedure. The established goals of the director were: to stress the faith of Job, not his physical anguish; to submerge the actors to the demands of the poem's imagery, music, and implicit ritual; to create figures larger than life in an attempt to match the importance of the argument; and finally, to make the production suitable for performance in church sanctuaries.

We rejected the realism of rags and ashes as unsuited for the church and likely to lend too much stress to Job the man. Then we examined art forms which exist in the church. Romanesque and Gothic sculpture and stained glass relate to specific periods of history. We did not wish to date the play. In the mosaic we found a medium that pushes back through time to the classic era and forward to the present. As a timeless art form, it gave us a universal garment in which to clothe Job, that ancient symbol of man's endurance and faith.

16
Head of a court dignitary. Mosaic at San Vitale, Ravenna.

Far from being crippling, these restrictions channeled our thoughts and challenged us to find a fresh concept for one of mankind's oldest stories. The drama, of course, may be done in a thousand different ways: as twentieth century man on the ashes of Hiroshima, or in overalls on the dung heap of a farm, or as *J. B.*, in a circus tent.

14

17
The women's chorus of *The Book of Job*.

18   A member of the chorus with mosaic make-up applied to only half of the face, demonstrating the necessity for integral costume and make-up design.

After we decided to use the mosaic form, the design plates were executed. To have conceived the costumes in the mosaic manner without carrying the motif onto the face, would have been to leave the image half finished, with a void for a face. It was necessary that the effect extend onto gloved hands, beards, wigs, and onto faces with a make-up mask.

Only after a design is rendered should thought be given to how the effect can be achieved. The vision must first be seen, then a way can be found to do it. To work with only what one already

¹⁹
Costume and make-up design for the male chorus of
The Book of Job. Cool blues and purples were used for
these four costumes to indicate their antipathy toward
Job.

²⁰
Shades of red and orange were used in the costumes of
the female chorus to reflect their empathic relationship
with Job.

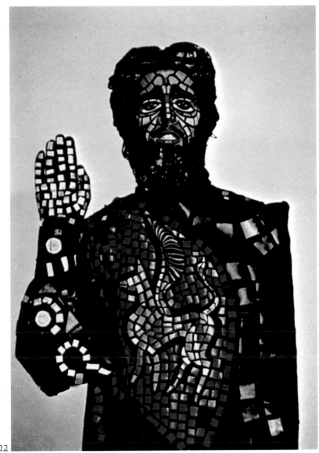

21
The costume and make-up design for Job showing his emblazoned cape. His basic robe was green implying his ever-verdant faith.

22

knows is to exclude what one may discover. Practicality, if it is used as an excuse for expediency, is the father of mediocrity. Practical factors must be examined for their specific limitations, of course, but even a limitation may become the threshold of new solutions.

An evaluation of all available materials may suggest an effect or provide a solution. For mosaics it was necessary to capture the jewel-like richness which emanates from the vibration of colors interlocked with one another. I examined fabrics to find which ones would shine and glow. Knowing that small glass chips catch and refract the light, the final choice was rayon satin, glued in squares on a matt cotton ground. The result was a shimmer of color as the actors moved. In the words of the reviewer for *The National Observer*, it created "a kaleidoscope of living mosaic."

23
Geometric compositions in *The Book of Job* were derived from the formal arrangements of figures in Byzantine mosaics.

Lewis Funke of the New York *Times* said: "The imagination is stirred . . . the eye magnetized. . . . It is as if the mosaics have come to life."

Invite your imagination to conjure the most exalted image and, once it has been captured in paint on paper, accept the challenge that it can be realized on the stage. Then go out and find a way to do it. This is the path to original solutions.

Finally, every decision about the production must be sieved through the directorial concept. This will influence all properties, the costumes, the make-up, the setting, and the very mood quality of the lights. When the visualization is compatible with the fundamental concept, it will even impose further guide-lines upon the director, reinforcing anew the original approach.

For *The Book of Job* the director immersed himself in the study of mosaic compositions. He found that geometric movement and rigid gestures seem to originate in the very squareness of the basic unit of all mosaics, the tiny tessera. Lack of depth and formal balance as seen in Hagia Sophia and in churches at Ravenna, suggested his stage picturization. He directed the actors to move in highly formal patterns, creating an atmosphere of ritual. Individual performers were totally submerged within the all-encompassing mosaic. The combined life force of the ensemble generated a multiplied power, magnifying the impact of the poem. The figures became monumental, approximating the importance of the literature. The very sound itself acquired the *quality* of a mosaic through the use of choral speaking, chanting, and singing, a further reflection of the blending of small pieces of glass to form a whole.

24
The facial expressions are enlarged by the make-up mask.

The ultimate validity of a design approach lies in its evocation of imagination. Hovering in the space between player and onlooker, suspended in time, upheld by attention, that fragile entity we call a play either lives or dies. Its evaluation rests with the viewer, and is voiced by the critic. Whitney Bolton of *The Morning Telegraph* could represent the hundreds of reviewers of *Job* when he wrote: "One sits enthralled as the beautiful language rolls on and the passion that was Job's unfolds. . . To sit there before those vivid colors, that evocative make-up, to hear the great words, the greatly human words, from the Old Testament as the chorales rise and the organ furnishes resonant accompaniment is to feel exaltation and pride."

At no point in theatre production is there a place for compromise. All decisions, however minute, must remain loyal to directorial and design concepts. These two standards form a true square against which all else may be lined up and measured. The resultant unity justifies all the effort. Nobody ever said it would be easy.

3

To Search for Sources

"Never let go of the main theme of the play when searching for variations in the scene. . . . approach it from all sides, surround it."

Gordon Craig
The Art of the Theatre

Costume design for Electra in Sophocles' *Electra*.

TO DESIGN a play is to set off on a safari, leaving the tamed tabby at home by the familiar fire. We hunt for live things, unfamiliar shapes, unknown forces, unpredictable actions. Ours is the adventure of pitting single wit against a greater power; ours is the desire to conquer. It is a dangerous safari, for the unknown lies ahead, and dense mystery closes in around us. It is the wondrous jungle and the strange sound and smell of it that lures us on. We are armed with anticipation. We know our equipment. With senses honed we respond to weird cries. These are animals never before seen; birds never dreamed.

Our guide is the playwright. He knows this terrain and has marked out our path. He suggests the game we may encounter; he does not shoot it for us. The director who suggested our safari, choosing the time and the place, has consulted the guide and knows the nature of the hunt. He has advised us to bring back a rare creature that has been scented and tracked but not seized. And when we find this elusive beast, we are to study his habitat, his food, and his environment. Once he is captured, his life must be sustained, for this is a safari for the living, with no place for the dead. Nor are we sent for known animals, for the commonplace. This is a journey for the unusual.

The scope and intensity of this safari determine the richness of the artist's inspiration. The more penetrating the search, the more complex the product.

It is first necessary to establish and examine some of the more common methods of stalking a design. The design approaches and categories I wish to explore are: selected realism, suprahuman expression, inspiration from flora and fauna, and the interpretation of existing art forms. This is not meant to be an exhaustive classification, but only to illustrate trails of creative search.

Selected realism is a simplified arrangement of carefully chosen details taken from the environment. When these details are changed in line or shape, intensifying their significance, the new form is stylized realism. Since it is not the purpose of this book to deal with naturalism, or even with obvious realistic design problems and solutions, nature will serve only as a source and a springboard.

It was my director's desire to strip our production of Arthur Miller's *The Crucible* of all realistic trappings, and to present the players in a timeless aspect as creatures captured in their own self-created hell, watching and helplessly participating in fanatical destruction. Faces alone were individually follow-spotted. The drama was enacted before a silhouetted frieze of the other members of the community. Costumes retained the period, with gray rather than white collars, and with red accents on the girls for psychological implication. The director wanted the people who were responsible for the nightmare of suspicion to become watching images of distrust and fear. Studying the faces of people photographed in the grip of emotional hatred, I found that the muscles contorted the mouth and the eyes, suggesting hard demoniacal masks. These became the faces of Salem. Patterns of hate were painted in gray, over a pale base.

Costume designs for *The Crucible:* Ezekial Cheever, John Proctor, Elizabeth Proctor, Thomas Putnam, Goody Putnam.

26

27

Final scene of *The Crucible*, with Elizabeth Proctor lighted against the dark tableau of the watching villagers.

A second example of a design approach using selected realism occurred in our production of *Don Quixote of la Mancha* by Arthur Fauquez. Here the challenge was to present two worlds: one, the vast, sun-bleached, garlic-scented Spain of Sancho, and the other, Quixote's boundless realm of illusion. To understand the Don's world of ideals, it is necessary not to see it from Sancho's point of view; it would be too easy to look and laugh. Both worlds must be perceived. This principle was pursued in the make-up by basing it on nature, selecting and idealizing facial characteristics. Another shaping factor was the decision to try to evoke the deep-engrained images of Gustave Doré, whose vision has influenced so many generations to his own understanding of the pathos and triumph of the mad knight and his loyal friend.

Detail from a Gustave Doré illustration of *Don Quixote*.

28

Don Quixote in the opening scene of the play by Arthur Fauquez.

29

23

30

Make-up plan for Brando Notcouth in *The Great Cross-Country Race* by Alan Broadhurst.

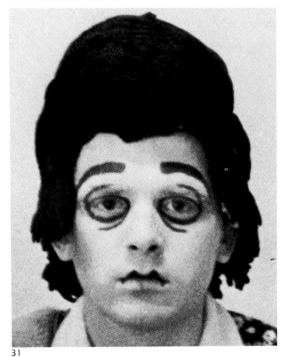

31

A realization of the Brando make-up.

The Great Cross-Country Race, a retelling by Alan Broadhurst of the tale of the tortoise and the hare, presents another variation of selected realism. Animals talk, people do not. It is the

animal world that communicates to us, while the "people-talk" is unintelligible both to the animals and the audience. To execute walking, talking animals calls for accurate selection and styling of

Make-up plan for Sophia, sister to Brando.

32

Sophia Notcouth complete with yarn hair in rollers.

33

34

35

Make-up plan for Maude and George, the Soppy Dates.

36

Facial types are delineated by use of black line, without the use of shading. Yarn wigs further emphasize a puppet-like quality.

detail. (What could be more distasteful than a man-sized squirrel covered with squirrel pelts?) It follows that humans in the same production should also be highly styled. Deprived of communication, watched with curiosity by kibitzing animals, the people were directed as unreal, puppet-like creatures. Faces were pale, with caricatured features painted on in black lines.

Yarn wigs further detached them from reality. By the simple use of line applied to the actor's face as if to a blank canvas, great facial variety was achieved. The soppy dates, for example, mooned about with love-sick eyes and painted smirks while Brando and Sophia surveyed the world with sulky indifference.

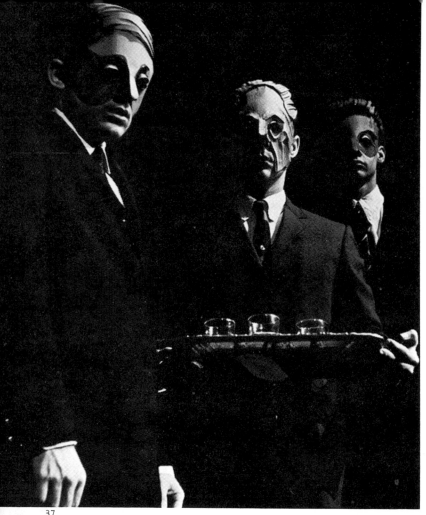

In considering the principle of selected realism, the mask should not be overlooked. From prehistoric time to the present day, it is capable of creating a great sense of mystery and awe. Gordon Craig felt "the mask is the only right medium of portraying the expressions of the soul as shown through the expressions of the face." Some modern plays demand masks. They are, of course, vital to Eugene O'Neill's *The Great God Brown*. The major characters wear masks which they often remove, indicating the public aspects of their personalities. I used the half-mask, executed in the medium of paper sculpture (not to be confused with the soggy bulk of papier-maché!). The sharp lines of the scored and bent water color paper translated the facial contours into the simplified planes of heightened realism. The texture

37
The butler and Dion's sons wearing paper sculpture masks in *The Great God Brown* by Eugene O'Neill.

Dion in the make-up of his real self, holding the satyr-like mask of his public self.   38

39
Paper sculpture mask for Margaret.

of the paper created a skin-like surface. By carrying the design over the crown of the head by means of cut-paper hair, a complete transformation took place. Tension between the cheek-bone and the crown kept the mask taut, made a smooth transition to the cheeks, and left the mouth free. When the masks were painted to match the make-up base, the effect of change was instantaneous. The masks, coated with plastic adhesive, were lightweight and extremely durable.

40
Paper sculpture mask for Brown's secretary.

41
Dion's second mask, which has become more diabolic with the passage of time.

42 Cybele, an earth-goddess, wearing the mask of a prostitute.

The hard mask is objectionable except when it is an organic part of the play. It eliminates the mobility of the actor's face, it muffles the voice, and unless superbly and subtly made (as in the Noh drama), it becomes monotonous. Breathing is impaired; the weight is tiring. And even in the case of the half-mask, joining with the face is inevitably awkward.

The make-up mask is generally a far more useful device. The actor's features are enlarged, not submerged, and facial communication is intensified. Oriental theatre—India's Kathakali, Japan's Kabuki, and China's Peking Opera—has used such stylized make-up for centuries. It is indeed strange that for its masks the modern Western theatre usually turns to the hard mask of the Greeks or the half-mask of the Commedia dell' Arte. It is the make-up mask that is seldom assimilated by our theatre.

With rare exceptions, such as *Tobacco Road* bedded down on Broadway in tons of actual dirt, naturalism is now by-passed in favor of selected realism. The selection of realistic detail is the first step of the artist in bringing design-order to the infinite variety offered by nature. The elimination of extraneous matter itself makes a statement and enables the idea to emerge. The selection and visual underlining of concepts is an elemental duty of the theatre designer.

Since the primitive painters of Altamira and Lascaux, the world of nature has furnished the artist with inspiration. In the same way that the cave artist reduced his animals to simple planes and fluid lines, so the theatrical designer who seeks to create an animal must select and translate dominant characteristics.

43

The Fox in *Reynard the Fox* by Arthur Fauquez.

44

28

45

The actor's features merge into those of the porcupine in *Reynard the Fox.*

46

Familiarity with the animal's features, movements and habits is the point of beginning. Style and silhouette are then translated into line, color and fabric. Translation is essential. Attributes such as fine-haired fur must be re-expressed in a larger medium so the *quality* of fur comes across. The effect is completed when the actor captures the vitality and gesture of the animal by observing and mastering a stylization of his movements. Without the wedding of mime to visualization the result will be the lowest form on the theatrical totem, a man in an animal suit.

The directorial concept for Arthur Fauquez's version of *Reynard the Fox* was to reveal the foibles of man through the antics of animals. When possible, the animals were sketched and studied first hand, and then salient animal features were re-interpreted into fabrics. The actor's face became a painting surface with colors and lines blending into the costume.

A svelte tuxedo front gave the suggestion of the white throat of the red fox. His red and white face thrust out to the tip of his organdy chops. Of organdy also was his tail, springing from the body on a wire frame and dancing above his quick-footed, black-slippered step.

In the porcupine, the light pink of the eye and chop area gave the essence of the animal's face. The nose was broadened above sharp teeth which were painted on the upper lip. The edges of the actor's face blended into the surrounding quills. Padding on the shoulders extended down the back, ending in a dragging tail. When the player adopted a slow, side-shuffling gait, the transformation took place, causing a reviewer for a Cape-town, South Africa, paper to ask: "*Where* did you get that six-foot porcupine?"

The king of beasts, Noble the lion, is best characterized by his massive mane. Translated into a tangle of half-inch strips of golden organdy, it constituted the major portion of his costume. With the same colors in the make-up mask, leonine features were captured by the angle of the eye, the width of the nose and the chops. By using the make-up mask, the actor maintained absolute mobility, and his expressions were enlarged, not obscured.

Rev. Epinard, the porcupine in *Reynard the Fox*, displays a bristling silhouette.

47

48

Noble the lion, in *Reynard the Fox*. The mobility of the face is enlarged by the make-up mask, exaggerating his react the discovery, smell, and taste of camembert cheese.

49

The color of the make-up blends into the costume elements, creating a unified effect.

As a prelude to one of his pranks, Reynard begs a blessing from the Rev. Epinard.

50

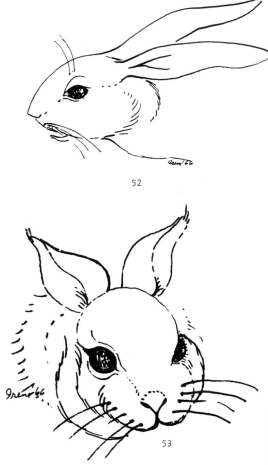

52

53

Mr. Fleet, a hare, flatters Mrs. Warren, a matronly rabbit in *The Great Cross-Country Race*, by Alan Broadhurst.

51

The Great Cross-Country Race calls for animals also, including that coil-spring of jack-legged activity, the hare. To the simple lines of the body were added proportional ears and tail, exaggerated feet, and knobby-knees and heels. The face was styled into planes. With bright-eyed insolence and buck-toothed consumption of food and drink, the fatuous hare bounded through the race in a cloud of braggadocio to the fabled photo-finish.

Mrs. Rabbit is shorter and stockier than her arrogant brother. Her maternal roundness was ex-

pressed in a net pouf on her stomach. Net cheeks were attached to her headdress. Her face was interpreted in curved lines.

For the badger, another solution was found to the problem of showing a rotund animal with short fur. A cocoon of net and organdy lightly rode upon a hoop suspended from the waist, moving freely with the body. Slits allowed the arms to partly emerge, creating the effect of short legs. The white line on the face extended over the head and down the back to the tip of the tail. The flat-

Mr. Basket, a basset hound, serves as translator between the animals and the people in *The Great Cross-Country Race*.

Sett, a badger, supervises the great race.

headed look was achieved by a horizontal hoop. Fat fingers and sharp claws completed this efficacious earth-burrowing animal.

In designing a dog, one must first determine what breed and which dog. The playwright of *The Great Cross-Country Race* specifies that Mr. Basket is a basset. Specific sketches of a basset hound revealed a series of down-drooping lines, particularly above and below the eyes. With weighted, flopping velvet ears, a turned-up wired tail, and enlarged paws, man's most ubiquitous friend was ready to serve the actor and the play.

57
Costume and make-up design for Calaban in Shakespeare's *The Tempest*.

58
Mr. Paddle, a water rat, looks through the cattails by the river bank in *The Great Cross-Country Race*.

From beneath round, bright eyes, the long nose of the rat was extended by a line from the high cheek bone to beneath the actor's nose, where rolled organdy moustaches drooped in a further extension of the line. The long slinky tail accented the slithering rat movement. A slight pink belly and acute ears softened his image.

Moving away from overt, obvious animals, Calaban in *The Tempest*, who has characteristics of man and beasts and the elements, offers an example of further stylization. Shakespeare describes him: "A freckled whelp . . . a man or a fish . . . legged like a man, and his fins like arms . . . a thing of darkness." His mother was "a blue-eyed hag." These images suggest the frog, the fish, the night, and blue-eyed evil. In view of these references, why is he traditionally portrayed as a bestial caveman? Calaban is not without wistful qualities. He fears being pinched.

Mr. Sloe, the tortoise, passes the water rat at a checkpoint in *The Great Cross-Country Race.* 59

60
Actors observe an ancient tortoise in the Houston Zoo.

He responds to the innocent lure of Miranda. He loves to be stroked and to drink water with berries in it. He is moved by music to gentle dreams. Why could he not have his mother's blue eyes? Using the freckles of the frog, a whimsical headdress, and a trailing cerise lined tail from the fish (to serve as rain-cover for Trinculo), our Calaban appeared as a potential man, bewitched into an unreal shape.

Turning to reptiles as a design source, the tortoise in *The Great Cross-Country Race* presented a formidable challenge. This marvel of nature must have a shell light enough for an actor to carry around on his back, large enough to conceal him when retracted, and strong enough to hold the hefty weight of a Badger at the opening of the play. The constructional problems were solved with fiberglass. Hooped fabric on arms and legs gave cumbersome bulk. The make-up, blending into a reptilian beaked nose and wrinkled mouth, combined with the costume to give the actor the mien and the restrictions of an actual tortoise. In such garb, the actor genuinely understood why the tortoise moves as he does!

61

A wistful woodsprite peers beneath her pearled antennae.

62

Moth in *A Midsummer Night's Dream.*

63

Designers also turn to insects for inspiration. In our overeseas touring production of *Reynard the Fox*, wood sprites with fanciful eyes and antennae were interpolated to change the seasonal settings in view of the audience. *A Midsummer Night's Dream* introduces Moth and Cobweb. Our Moth was presented in the vivid colors of a butterfly, with transparent wings of silk and gelatin. Cobweb was derived from the delicately designed architecture of the spider. On the filmy drape of a transparent cape the weblines were painted, extending onto the face. A touch of mystery was supplied by an elaborate jeweled design on the breast.

Shakespeare turns directly to plant life for Mustardseed and Peaseblossom. The mustard seed is proverbially tiny, but sharp and power-packed. These characteristics were interpreted by an acid yellow costume with fire-red spots, darting wings, and militant spiked antennae. Peaseblossom raised a pink-budded head above tendrilled hands and feet, weaving and swaying in an enchanted forest.

64

Cobweb in *A Midsummer Night's Dream.*

Peaseblossom serves as part of the wakening forest in *A Midnight Summer's Dream.*

65

The foregoing designs are direct stylizations from nature, but they need not always be so deliberate. The world of nature is open to the theatrical artist to interpret and to apply to less obvious characters. The legend of the origin of *aragoto* make-up for the Kabuki states that it came from the study of a peony petal. Although this has no seeming relation to the rough athletic figures on whom it is used, it does not invalidate the

freshness of the concept. Later I will present a more abstract design approach based on nature, identifying the tutor of Sophocles' *Electra* with the resurgence of hope epitomized by a growing plant.

In our production of *A Midsummer Night's Dream*, the director decided that since the action principally occurs in a forest, the denizens of the woods in their mastery and beauty should be given

66

Working drawing for Snout the Tinker whose design is based on the Vulturine guinea fowl.

primacy. I pored over books on trees, mosses, ferns, mushrooms, and birds. I assigned to each character in the play, except members of the court, a bird counterpart. My choices were based on color, line, and type. Two basic categories were the workmen of Athens and the enchanted beings of the forest. The rude mechanicals were aligned with the short, waddling water fowl—except for Snout, the taciturn tinker, who was modeled on the vulturine guinea fowl. With bald pate, scrawny neck and a shaggy garment, he scowled above his "wall."

For such an exotic creature as Titania, birds of paradise became the prototype. Elements of the lyre bird and the King of Saxony bird were included, combining colors of moss green, teal, and coral.

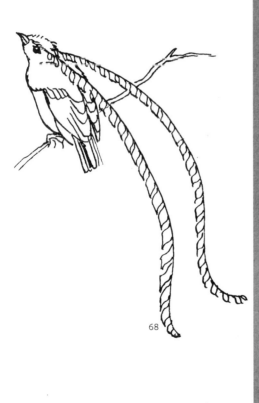

68

Costume and make-up design for Titania in *A Midsummer Night's Dream.* 69

Oberon and Titania's dance of reconciliation 72
in Act 4 of *A Midsummer Night's Dream*
was choreographed in the manner of the
mating dance of birds.

70

Oberon's counterpart was the grouse, whose
fluffed ruff and distended tail spikes were re-stated
in a draped cowl, spiked collar, and ribbed wings.
His colors were the shades of night.

Shakespeare structures this comedy around four
dimensions of love: courtly love (Theseus and
Hyppolyta), puppy love (the four young lovers),
parodied love (Pyramus and Thisby), and physical love. Illustrating the latter, Titania and Ober-

71 Costume and make-up design for Oberon in *A Midsummer Night's Dream.*

73 Puck, his make-up derived from the Masked Tanager, impishly observes, "Lord, what fools these mortals be."

74

on were directed to adopt movements of their birds as they appear in the mating dance.

The masked tanager identifies with the harlequinesque caprice of Puck, and provided him with a black "half-mask" with feathered horns, and just a hint of wings. Puck serves as the impish, roguish slave of Oberon. Mischievous and mysterious, he was clearly separated from the mortals of the play.

Puck in *A Midsummer Night's Dream.* 75

76
Tiecelin, a crow, the royal registrar in *Reynard the Fox*.

Tiecelin the crow, in *Reynard the Fox*, was a more direct representation of a bird. The make-up mask, with yellow on the beak, accomplished the illusion of a protruding bill. With padded breast and rump, claw feet, and careful mimicry of a crow, the actor captured the very essence of the bird.

When an artist in any field succeeds in making a statement involving several levels of experience and in capturing elements of timeless appeal, the result is called a work of art. Works of art so produced may serve as inspiration to artists working in other media. Shelley's poetic response to

77
Sculpture on the Royal portal of Chartres Cathedral.

Male Saint   Saint Paul   Female Saint.

Costume and make-up design for Saint Paul and the Chorus of Saints.

Aeschylus' lost but legendary tragedy of *Prometheus Unbound* was his own masterpiece by the same name. Keats' *Ode on a Grecian Urn* was inspired by the craft of an unknown Greek potter. The Duc de Berry's *Book of Hours* influenced Laurence Olivier's great motion picture, *Henry V*. Art history offers the theatrical designer a limitless range of stimulation, provided his imaginative response to the work of art can be properly wedded to the play at hand.

The Book of Job production, already explored, is an example of theatrical assimilation of the mosaic art form.

Gothic sculpture was chosen as appropriate to *Romans by Saint Paul* because it has a definite association with the early church. Orlin Corey's arrangement as a sermon-cantata seeks to sound the magnificent language of this "logic-poem" of Christian doctrine, stressing St. Paul's passion and affirmation of faith.

Built-up shoes, elongated fingers, and heightened foreheads exaggerated the vertical line of the players, making them stand "tall in faith." The sense of sculpture was enriched by bordered trim in bas-relief. Strong side lighting shadowed deep folds in the robes. Monochromatic colors were

79

Side-lighting on the figures in *Romans by St. Paul* altered them into cold stones, or cast gold.

chosen from the warm hues of stone mellowed in the late afternoon sun. These colors were carried onto the face; black lines delineated features, pushing the eyes and eyebrows upward in proportion to the high forehead.

The physical difficulties of this creation on the actor were seen early in rehearsal. They soon learned to maneuver on the six-inch raised buskins. When "break-time" was called, however, and players forgot they were saints, they toppled like bowling pins. Yet in twenty-one performances on twenty-one different sets of steps and levels of churches and cathedrals during the first tour, no one "fell from grace."

The effectiveness of the statuesque figures was reflected in numerous reviews in which the following from Britain are typical: "With a certain incredulity we saw . . . men as trees walking . . . truly awesome. The cadences of the Authorized Version rose and fell with a compelling power that positively made the scalp prickle. An experience of a kind of living scripture that one would not willingly have missed. . . There were giants in the earth." (*The Tablet*, London) ". . . Paul emerges as a human being. This is not only quite unlike any theatre one has seen before, it has tremendous, and at times almost frightening force." (*The Daily Post*, Liverpool)

80
80
Transparent walls reveal a wondrous garden in a setting for Moliere's *The Miser*.

Two art forms merged in the designing of *The Miser* by Molière. The directorial concept contrasted the Miser, obsessed by his own greed, with all the beauty of life about him. As setting I used the pastel hues of a rococo garden. For costumes and make-up I referred to the Commedia dell' Arte, styling its half-masks into make-up. Harpagon, for example, was based on Pantalone, his face was marred by greed and avarice, illustrating the timeless lunacy that possessions bring security. Unaware of the beautiful garden world around him, he thought only of his buried treasure.

81
A half-mask for the commedia dell 'arte character Pantalone.

The miser Harpagon, with make-up derived from the Pantalone mask.

82

45

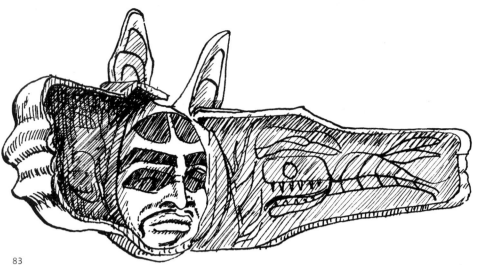

83
Carved wooden deer mask of the Northwest Coast Indians.

In the pre-publication version of Arthur Fauquez's *Don Quixote of La Mancha*, the mad knight's horse and Sancho's donkey were narrators of the play. It is baffling enough to make a one-manpower horse, capable of charging in a joust with a rider on his back, let alone to contrive a way for him to speak! The art form I turned to was the mask of the Northwest Coast Indians. These intricately carved animal masks are divided

Actors and designer studying horses preliminary to the creation of Rosinante in *Don Quixote of la Mancha*.
84

Actor encased in wire and wood framework for Rosinante.
85

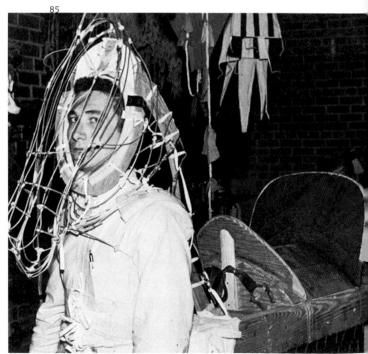

The designer covers the frame of the horse's head with porous cheese cloth, to allow breathing and visibility. 87

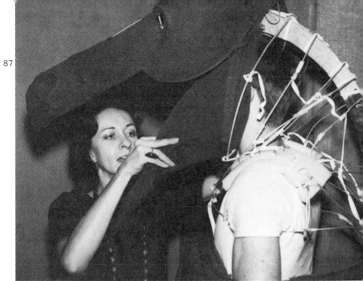

86
Don Quixote mounted on Rosinante. The decorated reins are attached to the arms of the actor animating the horse.

When the horse narrates the play, he opens his "visor" revealing the spirit of Rosinante.
88

into sections, opening out like flower petals. Inside is revealed a face of the animal spirit. I positioned the actor's head inside the throat of the horse. His arms formed the bridle, so that when he wished to speak he could raise the top of the horse's head like a visor. His make-up indicated the spirit of Quixote's faithful nag.

Costume designs for the workmen in Dorothy Sayers' *The
Zeal of Thy House.*

89

One of the most intriguing problems a designer can confront is the challenge to create with physical means a metaphysical being. Mask is the ancient and ageless answer of the theatre. It is interesting to consider its effect upon man. Richard Southern analyzes this phenomenon in his book *The Seven Ages of Theatre:* "What does a mask do to the man? Two things: it takes away from the person we know (it can even take away humanity). And it invests the wearer with something we do not know, but which is aweful and non-human, a god or a devil. The mask rehabilitates the player's face." He goes on to say that masks serve to suppress man and allow him to assume a new personality.

Instead of being hemmed in by an insoluble problem, the designer is suddenly freed of dependence on the individual features of the actor, freed of the recognizable scale of the body. The whole world of invention is open, and he is limited only by the scope of his own observation and imagination. The only other restrictions come from the play itself, and from the goal set by the director. When the aesthetic compass is set, the direction of research is determined.

In *The Zeal of Thy House*, Dorothy Sayers

dramatizes the story of the building of Canterbury Cathedral. Among the workaday world of the carpenters and stonemasons and monks, she introduces three archangels, Michael, Gabriel, and Raphael. The problem is to set them apart convincingly from their flesh and blood companions, giving them a superhuman eminence. Visits to medieval cathedrals had left us with the memory of glowing windows, ribbed with dark tracery. From these I selected strong color and linear qualities. In the early glass, faces are painted in sterotyped, impersonal formats; the features are heavily outlined. A light base make-up was used, and with features arbitrarily painted on the face, the angels became stark and impersonal. Artists of the middle ages assumed that angels have wings because they were sighted in the sky. They proceeded to feather the angels in vibrant colors. In the space age are we to limit angels to white feathered wings? A fanciful symbol of flight should suffice. Our archangels "flew" by means of twinkling cellophane strips and sheer net. Shimmering satins were juxtaposed on the costumes, setting up color vibrations, so that the glow of stained glass was realized. All was overlaid with tracery. In this way the angels were set apart from the earthen-hued world.

90

Costume and make-up design for the archangel Michael
in *The Zeal of Thy House*.

91

Costume and make-up design for the archangel Gabriel
in *The Zeal of Thy House*.

The three archangels: Gabriel,
Raphael, and Michael.   92

93

Make-up designs for the three witches in *Macbeth*. They reflected characteristics of the prototypes assigned to them—the toad, the bat, and the cat.

Shakespeare frequently leavens his *dramatis personae* with characters who stand apart from the human level and assume superhuman powers. Some are good, and others, such as that malevolent trio, the witches in *Macbeth*, are evil. In our production, analysis pursued the idea of the emergence of evil in Macbeth's life. As he follows the bony-fingered way pointed by the witches, they become ever more real to him, while true reality recedes until he is lost in total illusion. From lines spoken by the weird sisters, or from objects venerated by them, came the clues for their visualization. The first witch was linked to the streaked cat ("brinded cat," and "Graymalkin") which she serves. The second was identified by the toad ("Paddock"). The third crone ("Harpier") was associated with a bat because of the hovering "through the fog and filthy air" and the deep darkness in which the action is immersed.

These same creatures are echoed by name in the cauldron scene of Act Four. Even the ingredients of the charmed potion suggest the palate and appetite of a cat, a toad, and a bat.

The actresses assigned to these roles explored the movements of their prototypes. They were given costume and stylized make-up elements to complete the image of subhuman creatures. Freed from the stereotype of ragged old women, they looked "not like the inhabitants of the earth," but like sinister and anti-human forces.

When T. S. Eliot conceived of Thomas à Becket's inner struggle in *Murder in the Cathedral*, he personified Becket's temptations in four Tempters. It is traditional to interpret these as realistic men. It was my director's desire to abstract them into supernatural beings. To accomplish this, I turned to the use of symbolic color and the make-up mask.

94 Costume and make-up design for Tempter I in *Murder in the Cathedral* by T. S. Eliot.

Tempter I represented the temptation of fleshly appetites.
95

Tempter One suggested sensual pleasure and presented a weak, dissipated face. The busy broken lines of his costume reflected a playboy flippancy. Pastel colors in sheer fabrics implied the shallowness of ephemeral pleasure.

96
Costume and make-up design for Tempter II, representing the temptation of legal power and monetary gain.

97
Costume and make-up design for Tempter III, presenting the aspect of power by physical strength.

From a cash-cold face, Tempter Two invited Becket to use monetary gain and political appointment to achieve earthly power. His robe of purple, gold, and red underlined the luxury he represented.

With a burst of sun against red, Tempter Three radiated the use of merciless physical force, embodying the brutality of the barons of England.

99

Tempter IV presents a skull-like face beneath the ornately jeweled mitre.

Thomas à Becket surrounded by the four tempters, abstracted projections of his own mind.

100

98

Tempter IV lured Becket with the mocking offer of calculated martyrdom.

Beneath his jeweled mitre, Tempter Four mocked Becket with the temptation of spiritual pride and forced martyrdom, leering an invitation to "the greatest treason: To do the right deed for the wrong reason."

The culminating stage realization was that of Becket, the man, surrounded by the surreal and terrible temptations of his own mind.

53

101

A raked stage pointed toward infinity provided the setting for *Electra* by Sophocles. Motifs of Minoan architecture appeared in the altar and palace gateway.

In the foregoing examples an attempt has been made to relate visual concepts to design sources. These have been categorized to show more or less pure examples. Of course, most design problems are more complex, particularly those evolving from plays of great universal significance. Sophocles' *Electra* is such a drama, plummeting to the depths of human experience. Our production of it is offered as an example of the synthesis of several sources of design.

Directorial analysis revealed that the play is woven of two major themes: the power of past evil and a divine justice which rights wrong. We treated the play as a drama of justice, not of matricide, as did Euripides in his version of the legend. Because of the primitive brutality in the play, our production was placed at the roots of Greek history, in the Minoan culture.

Edith Hamilton says that Greek tragedy brings before us the strangeness that surrounds us, the dark unknown our life is bounded by. The surrealists view life as existing on two levels: the revealed world of the visible, and a vague world of the subconscious. These two ideas were united in the visualization of the directorial concept: the cry of old evil for present justice.

The sacred horns of Mycenae at the Palace of Knossos on the island of Crete.

102

54

We treated *Electra* as a memory play. The events of the past and the events of the present linked in the mind of Electra. To create a background of mysterious infinity, a raked marble white stage with black lines of diminishing perspective was overhung with a coarse net. Symbolizing a woven web of the past, it cradled the severed head of Agamemnon. The sacred horns of Crete lifted up the offering at the altar. They also formed a crenellated crest above the gateway and its descending steps into the palace. The very shape of these horns later contributed to the basic movement of the actors in their performance of the ritual sacrifice.

To fit the players into this surrealistic setting, it was necessary to remember that the Greek tragic characters are not ordinary people, but extraordinary people simplified to essential characteristics. For this reason realism was used as the point of departure. Crucial details were selected for the make-up of Electra, Orestes, and the Chorus. As the complexity of the characters increased, so did the stylization.

Electra was portrayed as a Job-like figure, bowed down by the memory of her mother's enormous crimes. The earthen-hued women of the Chorus remembered and mourned with her.

An earthen-hued peasant chorus mourns with the black-clad Electra.

103

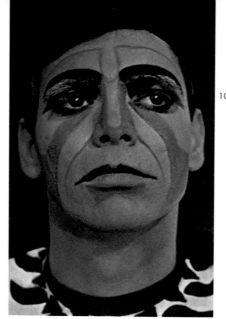

105 Orestes' make-up mask illustrates the method of selected realism.

Costume and make-up design for Electra's sister, Chrysothemes. She reflects the influence of her mother and the luxury of the corrupt court.

106

104

Orestes, as he returns to avenge his father's betrayal and murder.

Orestes revealed a grave responsibility to right the wrong done his father.

For the sister, Chrysothemes, another concept emerged in the make-up: the use of white to disguise inner reality. Reflecting the influence of her mother and the decadent luxury of the court, she resembled the polished marble of the palace.

A slave to the queen.

107

The serving women of the Queen were played as enigmatic, serpentine slaves. A degree of evil was implied by the make-up design and by the use of a reptilian red trim.

Slave-servants to Clytemnestra reveal growing aspects of evil.

108

109

Costume and ma
up design for Ae
thus in Sophoc
Electra.

Aegisthus, an ominous presense felt and feared throughout the play, brings a visage of cruel decadence when he finally makes his appearance.

110

Make-up chart for Aegisthus.

111

Aegisthus, described but not seen until the play is nearly over, must present the quintessence of sensual rot. His cruel face must make credible all the evil attributed to him.

112

Costume and mak
up design for Cl
temnestra.

The overlaying of evil with white climaxed with Clytemnestra, establishing the paradox that the greater the effort to disguise character, the clearer it becomes. Her make-up was a complete mask, a mask which cloaked and yet revealed, a face suitable to a character who would deserve murder by her own son. She was robed in white under a jangling eastern crown topped by the sacred horns of Mycenae. Draped with a bejewelled serpent, she stood in sharp contrast to the stark black figure of Electra. Here was a dramatic reversal of the traditional use of white for heroines, black for villains. Colors have strong psychological associations, but when new relationships are established, their associations may change. There is no reason to be rutted into stereotypes.

113
Clytemnestra's make-up suggests purity by the use of white, but succeeds in accenting her underlying evil.

Make-up chart for Clytemnestra. 114

115

Costume and make-up design for the tutor, the ancient friend and guide to Electra.

Justice, in the person of the ancient tutor, carried a leaf-adorned staff and wore a tree-like headdress, suggesting the evergreen leaf of truth. As he returned for the day of execution, his face contrasted with the decadence he discovered. Patterned with age, a venerable representative of the truth, he saw with clear eyes.

The dark primitive roots of man attracted my first research for this production. With no particular character in mind, I delved into books on the art of native Africa, ancient Assyria, Sumeria, and the Mayans. In search of the exotic and sensuous, I studied Indonesian design. Last of all, the Minoan culture was explored for details of architecture and costume.

Steeped in this esoteric research, I began the designs. There is no way to establish the true course of the creative process. Somehow from the deeps of experience which exist in all of us, images surface and are united with the undertaking of the moment. An Indonesian snake necklace was placed around Clytemnestra's neck. Her crown was inspired from a Sumerian queen's headdress. She walked under an Assyrian umbrella. The tutor carried a staff based on a Mayan sceptre and wore a headdress, shaped like a gnarled tree stump, taken from a Sumerian statue. The resultant metamorphosis of mysterious forms magnified characters, made them larger than time. Ceremonially thrust within a surrealistic setting evocative of infinity, they succeeded in presenting the once and present horror as one.

All areas of inspiration are fair game for the artist of the theatre. It is necessary that stereotypes be demolished, and that vision and observation be all-encompassing. Selection of details determines the final form, and must be guided only by the highest goal of the stage, the optimum truth of theatre.

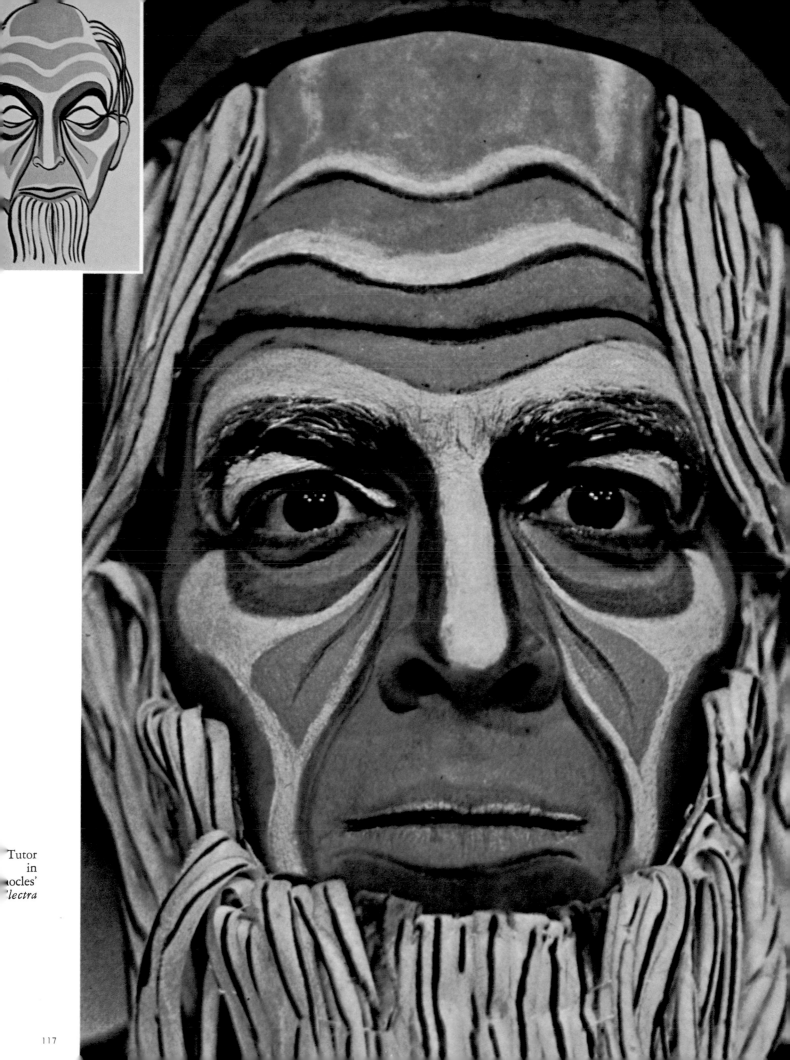

Tutor
in
[S]ocles'
[E]lectra

117

4

To Transform the Actor

". . . the business of the costumes is to reveal
and ennoble the actor's part, as the actor's
business is to fill them; together mutually they
define and illuminate each other."

Stark Young
The Theatre

I T IS MY belief that make-up and costume design should not be separated. Knowledge of the personality of each character, supplied by the playwright, determines all decisions concerning line, color, and accessories of dress. Personality traits, which are also reflected in the face, should be included in the design plates.

The story is told of Abraham Lincoln that he once refused a man a certain appointment. When his friends questioned him about it, he said, "I didn't like his face." "But," they protested, "you can't turn a man down for a reason like that. He can't help the way he looks." Lincoln replied, "Show me a man who is forty years old who is *not* responsible for his face."

Faces record experience, mental and physical. The same experience shapes taste. Taste determines selection of clothes. Selection reveals character. And we are back to a summation of the whole man again. Costume and make-up are inseparable and indivisible. If unity is to prevail they must evolve from the same mind.

It is not only the whole man which concerns the costume designer, but how he appears in the stage picture. A costume should make a complete statement in itself. It must also carry on a conversation with the clothes around it. God forbid it be a quarrel, unless by intention! These ever-changing juxtapositions reveal an overall pattern, always communicating new information. For this reason a comprehensive costume chart should be laid out before starting individual plates. This chart serves as a "pre-production curtain call." Here we identify the major forces in the play, check the emotional evolution of the plot as revealed by color, and indicate the interrelation of people. Details follow.

A knowledge of period dress is important as a

Paul in the Everyman Players' production of *Romans*
St. Paul.

119
Preliminary costume chart for *The Merry Wives of Windsor*.

visual record of the vanity of man. To be a master of, and not a slave to, these infinite details is to reign over a vast treasure. Perhaps more important than a knowledge of period is the knowledge of cut. The riddle of fashion is solved by the techniques of cutting. Whatever may be imagined can be created.

A fresh look at available materials gives a new slant on costuming. This is required for the same reason research is done on a play: to maintain knowledge of what is available, and to learn how materials will perform. It is helpful to know how fabrics have been used before, unless knowing the rules makes one dependent upon them. In this prolific scientific age, plastics, synthetics, and new forms of familiar substances are developed every day. Keeping up with what is available, finding out where to get it, and discovering how to use it are all part of the theatre artist's business.

No matter where one lives, "creative shopping trips" should be made frequently through the local dime store, hardware shop, and lumber yard. Try to forget the original purpose for which an item is manufactured, and think, "What will this object do?"

It is said that an Eskimo artist before beginning to carve a piece of ivory will ask, "Who is that in there?" Don't let the clerks overhear you, but do try asking the question.

For example, the lowly plumber's friend, used for unstopping reluctant drains, makes an excellent self-supporting wig stand when a tuft of net is attached to the top. Would it not also become a row of fanciful flowers, which could be easily struck from the stage? Or make a sudden sign post? Attached to a wimple it could form the base of a fantastic headdress like those worn by natives of northern India, medieval in silhouette.

Notes kept on materials and their potential are useful buttresses to the memory. Regarding fabrics and trim, the following chart may serve as a guide. The categories are based on how the materials perform. Their use may be applied to costume, costume trim, properties, or set decor.

STIFFNESS:
>   wire (millinery, aluminum, stove, hoop)
>   buckram
>   cardboard
>   starch
>   crinoline
>   net
>   copper foil
>   aluminum sheeting
>   felt, felt stiffener
>   pipe cleaners
>   organdy

SOFTNESS:

(Lightweight)	(Heavyweight)
nylon chiffon	unbleached cotton sheets
cheesecloth	jersey, nylon and wool
crepe, rayon	wool crepe
	terry cloth
	lead-weighted fabrics

FURRINESS:
>   rugs, synthetic fiber, long pile
>   ruffled net
>   bunny cloth
>   angora wool yarn
>   Maribou feathers
>   organdy, cut into strips

CRISPNESS:

(Lightweight)	(Heavyweight)
silk organza	taffeta
nylon organdy	peau de soie
cotton-lined-with-net	
nylon net	

BULKINESS:
>   burlap
>   blankets, rayon, wool, cotton, felt
>   drapery fabrics
>   upholstery fabrics

TO REFLECT LIGHT:
>   sequins
>   cellophane
>   gelatins
>   plastics
>   glitter
>   lamé
>   satin
>   metallic paints

TO STICK:
>   rubber cement
>   airplane cement
>   epoxy
>   "Elmer's," "Sobo," etc.
>   laminating plastics

TO SCULPT:
>   papier maché
>   theatre mold
>   sculptofab
>   paper sculpture
>   screen wire

TO TEXTURE:
>   sawdust
>   theatre mold
>   jute
>   rope
>   chicken wire

The preceding chart establishes a backlog of physical information, and the problems to be solved can now be considered.

Each situation will suggest several types of materials. Choose the one that works best. For example, permanent finished cotton organdy provided solutions for the following problems, although none of these uses of this fabric would be considered "normal":

121

Similar strips, shaped and tacked in place on a wig base, created the elaborately coifed wigs of the Louis XIV period, as used by Cleante in *The Miser*.

120

122

Cut in half-inch strips, organdy furnished the ruff for Dandy-Lion and also the beard for King Onion. The curling white "roots" of hair and beard swept from chin to ankle, and were topped by a crown derived from the onion seed pod.

The same method created the massive mane for the lion seen on page 31.

Porcupine quills made from thrice-folded triangular spears of organdy, bristled with prickly defiance;

123

organdy folded in the same way became wigs and beards for the men in *The Book of Job*. It was attached to a wimple base and was organized by

124

tacking threads; fastened with spirit gum, rolls of bias organdy also became the whiskers for a rat.

This crisp, lightweight fabric lends itself to an infinite variety of things, appearing as bear fur, fox tails, Spanish moss, foliage, and the hair of saints!

125

Romans by St. Paul serves as an example of a further search for appropriate materials to realize a total design. Wigs and beards were created by rolling bias cut organdy into tiny spaghetti-shaped tubes. Arranged and sewn in place, they were then sprayed with clear lacquer to set the raw edges. The bias cut of the garments demanded extra wide fabric which would drape well. Cotton sheet blankets answered this need. As the actors moved, weighted hems always guaranteed the return of deeply vertical shadows. Stone chiseled details of hair and elaborate jeweled trim were simulated by rolled organdy, heavy felt cut-outs, rope, and halved cork balls. Every material was chosen for its contribution to the desired effect of sculpture.

To represent fur with fabric one must first determine whether it is short, stiff, mangy, silky, or long and flowing.

The marmot, a rotund member of the rodent family, has short brown fur, shading into gold at the ends. A double layer of brown and gold net formed a round cocoon. The transparency and bouyancy of the fabric created a short legged, fluffy ball.

A coarser fur, suitable for a rambunctious bear, was made from looped strips of organdy.

Brun the bear in *Reynard the Fox.*
127

126
Lendore the marmot, a rotund member of the rodent family for the Fauquez play, *Reynard the Fox.*

Ysengrin, the unscrupulou
wolf in *Reynard the Fox*

The mangy fur of a cowardly wolf was translated into shaggy strips of outing flannel.
His ears, of course, were organdy.

129

The egg-loving hedgehog
in *The Great Cross-Coun-
try Race.*

The hedgehog is covered with stubby prickles. He was textured with gathered rows of
net, interspersed with pipe cleaners, sewn to an organdy base.

130
The phenomenon of light filtered through stained glass windows.

Light, filtering through stained glass onto cathedral stones, was our inspiration for the costumes of the women's chorus of T. S. Eliot's *Murder in the Cathedral*. A timeless witness, observing and interpreting the action, they appeared to be both women of Canterbury and an organic part of the cathedral. Vivid reds and oranges were used beneath sheer night-blue chiffon, causing an iridescent glow-and-shadow in movement. This type of overlay has infinite possibilities.

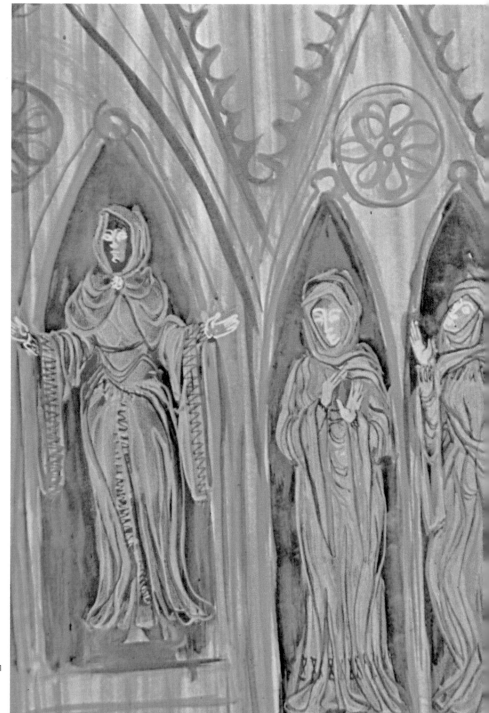

Costume and make-up design for the womens' chorus in *Murder in the Cathedral*. The costumes were designed to capture the effect of light sifted through stained glass onto stone.

131

132
The women of the chorus in Eliot's *Murder in the Cathedral*, serving as an ever-present witness to the tragedy.

Each fabric has a personality and will of its own. To learn its habits, its character, its method of communication, is to find an ally. It is a poor artist who does not know his materials, for these are what his visions must be made of. Sparked with imagination these simple dry goods may become the raiment of demons, the mantles of kings, and even the garments of gods.

Though billions of people in the world bear swirling designs on their finger tips, there is enough variation for an individual to be identified by his own fingerprint. Are the possibilities for variation in a face any less? We all have a lot in common, such as two eyes, a nose, and a mouth. Unlike the Helen Hokinson cartoon in which a little lady seeing a group of sailors, asks, "How do you tell each other apart?" we can and do identify each other.

In view of this infinite variation, I can never

understand the presumption of · the barefaced school of acting. The mathematical chance that an actor's own face will possess the physical characteristics demanded by a playwright for a specific role must be astronomical.

If it is granted that the author makes careful psychological distinctions in his characters and moves them with subtly contrasting motivation and ideals, then it must follow that he believes each variation is important. Character is always revealed physically. Our faces are records of the time that has passed through us. How we use our time determines the very contour of our visage. This facial evidence is too important for an actor to ignore.

Nor is make-up application a matter to be left to personal whim and technique. If the production is to maintain total unity, a definite style of

75

make-up must be followed by the entire cast. In previous times when actors or opera stars convened for a performance, each brought his own wardrobe, and all their personal tastes collided on the stage in one grand mélange. It is surprising to see this archaic practice still carried on in stage make-up, not just on the amateur level, but professionally in the New York and London theatres. If the star who insists on a solid socket of blue eye make-up had her way, the stages would be filled with blue-eyed death's heads. Only when make-up comes under the supervision of one person will such chaos be eliminated. Ideally, the costume designer should plot the make-up. The costume is a statement of character based on research and consultation with the director. Obviously the face should be an extension of this same information.

Make-up research is available to all. Archives of experience walk by every day, everywhere. What a wealth of material is around us, both face to face and in photographs! An organized file of notations and cut-outs of people is an infinitely useful source for designer and actor. Here one may file the haunted face of a soldier whose eyes reflect death observed; the innocuous advertisement-conformed face of the "beauty," correct in every outer detail; the face of the business man, horizontally lined by external pressures and internal tensions; the soft, well-tended, carefully fertilized face, with stylishly coifed gray hair accented by the glitter of hard eyes; faces contorted by the emotion of hated; the haggard, drawn, prematurely-aged Iagos, playing false to "friends," reflecting distaste for self and mankind. All of these and thousands more are ours for the seeing, faces which reveal, faces which conceal.

But is it the countenance alone that marks us off as individuals? Are not the clothes we wear also a part of this communication of self to others? A person looks the way he looks because he is the way he is and because he chooses what he has chosen. Can we do less on the stage? Every decision of dress, accessory, hair style, and make-up must be weighed in relation to the character. The director's insights are crucial in these value judgements.

Approached in this way, costuming becomes a boon, not a curse, to the character development of the actor. The all-American slouch does not necessarily suit every play. Elements such as corsets, capes, paunches, wigs, trailing gowns, and swords are, indeed, restrictions, but they are the very restrictions which separate one character from another, and one period from another.

This does not always mean that an actor will be comfortable. Was Queen Elizabeth I comfortable in her court attire at Westminster? Was Richard III comfortable in his deformity? Is a ballet dancer au point comfortable? What does comfort have to do with the price of character?

It is true, of course, that all of these elements —indeed, all staging devices—are useless until that magic moment when they are given life by an actor in exchange for the attention of the audience. All external forces are added to increase the effect on stage, to magnify the playwright's ideas.

In the first primitive stirrings of theatre, the individual added a mask, props, and music to intensify his performance. It is notable that in many of the great traditional dance theatres of the world,

Ken Holaman as Mr. Sloe, the tortoise 133

costumes have evolved which are directly opposed to ease of movement and body freedom. The Kathakali dancers of India have voluminous skirts and elaborate headdresses. Whether these costumes developed from religious traditions or out of an attempt to achieve the desired effect of performance, or both, their restriction contributes to the style of dance which evolved.

If there is to be a place for personal ego in the theatre, let it be sublimated into the pride of a mutual artistic integrity permeating the entire production.

A designer "feels" a costume subjectively within the framework of the concept. An actor must not only absorb the concept, but also add his personality to it. For as Hilton Edwards states, ". . . the mask of make-up is a dead thing, a mere painted grimace until its wearer makes it a part of himself . . . . the mask remains a mask until the images of the mind give it life."

I have included the statements of four players for an inside report on the wearing of integral costume and make-up. Their personal evaluation adds another dimension to understanding the philosophy of this design approach. Ken Holamon writes about his role as Mr. Sloe, a tortoise, in *The Great Cross-Country Race:*

"'Is it hard being a turtle?' My stock reply to this question was, 'What else can a person be with a shell on his back and the rest of his body encompassed in wire and cloth?'

"Most people laugh politely. What they fail to realize is that buried beneath the joke are basic truths. Just as there was a small actor beneath the large shell.

"The costume for Mr. Sloe sought to transform a lively, small-framed actor into a sluggish reptile of more than respectable proportions. In this bit of magic a great number of physical restrictions were imposed. The heavy shell forced my body into an uncomfortable 'question mark' shape, making it impossible to sit down off stage. My only form of relaxation came when I was placed on my back. But, like a turtle, I could not right myself without assistance. The remainder of the costume restricted me from all human activities, from coke to smoke.

"With few exceptions I rehearsed in costume. On the rare occasions when I did not, I found it beyond my ability to become Mr. Sloe. Even the voice was affected by the shell harness across my chest. The walk was impossible to recreate without the aid of the shell.

"I realized that there was no turtle in me. The

134 Gay Farley as Tiecelin, the crow

costume was filled with turtle qualities and yet it was not Mr. Sloe. The miracle of creation came in the spark of life caused by the union between actor and costume. Mr. Sloe was not the creation of either the actor or the costumier. He was truly the combination of turtle tendencies so obvious in the costume and so concealed in the actor.

"I had serious reservations about the three and three-quarters hours of nightly make-up and costuming necessary for a play of barely half that length. However, when the first child spontaneously reacted to my 'entrance' from beneath the shell, all qualms and misgivings evaporated.

" 'It must have been hell to wear that costume,' a friend remarked. Yes, I thought, but not half the hell of having to do the show without its assistance."

. . .

Gay Farley, for six years with The Everyman Players, played Tiecelin the crow, in *Reynard the Fox* for a three months' tour of South African cities.

"For days I had observed the sleek, intense bird called the crow. The sharp action, the quick run, and the keen look in the eye with the head cocked at an angle, all became part of my character. A stylization of these observations was necessary. I wanted to use only the most important symbols which would communicate Tiecelin to the audience. A natural portrayal could have resulted in

a rather comical character. Tiecelin is funny at times, but she certainly is not a comic.

"Although I felt confident that my movements were precise, that my voice was right for Tiecelin, that the inter-acting on stage with the other characters was alive, I knew that I was too conscious of myself acting as a crow. And, to be honest, I did not look too much like a bird.

"A week before the show opened, the costumes were completed and that exciting time of concealment came. I grabbed my sceptre and dashed to the mirror. The reflection was shocking. There stood the largest crow I'd ever seen. I looked at it for some time—at its large yellow feet, sleek body, glistening breast, and small black face. Suddenly I cocked my head to one side. The transformation was complete. I was still the actress, but the image in the mirror was an extension of myself.

"There were several disadvantages in Tiecelin's costume. The ears were covered and hearing was obstructed, affecting my sense of balance for a few days. I found it difficult to maneuver backstage because of the tail feathers and the large feet. However, with caution and familiarity with the costume, these problems were overcome.

"As rehearsals progressed I realized there were also advantages to this design. My vision was not impaired by a cumbersome hard mask, yet I gave the distinct impression of looking like a crow.

Costume design for
Harpagon the Miser 135

Facial expression was not lost. My movements became more natural. At last this crow and I were of the same mind and body. Whereas before I had felt outside myself and the character, I was now inside both. I was more confident of the precise effect being created.

"Another aspect appeared after the performance. When the make-up and costume were removed, the extension of myself was also shed. Tiecelin was no longer in existence. This is an extremely important part of acting, for the actress must know the foundation of herself. She cannot continue to play the role after the performance; if she does, on what base will she build new characters?"

. . .

George Bryan, associate director for *The Book of Job*, and veteran performer with the Everyman Players, writes of three of his roles:

"The business of the actor—with particular reference to myself—involves two processes, schizophrenic in themselves: how to erase *me* from my thinking in order to allow the playwright's *characterization* to evolve, and how to transform my experiences and sensibilities into stage realities which embody the author's intentions and the director's concept of the production. In both cases, as an actor, I am endeavoring to make a new being larger than myself, I am seeking to expand me beyond the frontiers of myself, and to do this, I need all the help I can get.

"As a creature of sometimes laughable meanness in a pastel garden peopled by Dresden-like china figurines, my task in the role of Harpagon the Miser in Molière's comedy was to soar to heights of monomaniacal obsession with imagined wrongs, contrasting forcefully with the beautiful, normal people of my household. I was to be a surrealistic character in a realistic world. Creativity was stymied by my own natural inhibitions. Then along came Irene Corey with her make-up mask, and I was so transformed that even my parents were unable to recognize me, and there was the solution. It was not *I* who was the raving pantaloon; it was the image which she had created. So much for inhibitions, but what about inspiration? One simply had to gaze admiringly at the romantic costumes of the other characters to appreciate the alien spirit of Harpagon, with his baggy, drab, grime-besoiled, formless suit which was crowned and dominated by scraggly, scruffy organdy hair and beard. The picture was completed by the addition of a putty proboscis, moles, and prominent veins in red and green. The Miser's basic posture was suggested by the designer's water color rendering of the costume and make-up, fertile ground for the imagination. The grasping gestures, the quick suspicious walk, and the carrion-carriage of the turkey buzzard were natural developments from that point, enthusiastically encouraged by the director.

George Bryan as
Rev. Epinard, the
136 Porcupine

George Bryan
as Eliphaz 137

"The role of the Reverend Epinard the porcupine in *Reynard the Fox* presented a different set of problems. The director had decided that the qualities of porcupine-ness were dramatically more important than those of preacher-ness, and the designer's costume presented an interesting and sometimes frustrating group of restrictions. The silhouette of the porcupine had been captured in the costume; the actor's task was simply to animate the silhouette properly, an undertaking which required a visit to the local porcupine. He was quite cooperative, and his slow, rolling movement seemed easy to imitate. However, changing the actions of a quadruped to those of a biped was harder than it looked. The great dragging tail, which reached from crown to floor—and several feet behind—had to be activated, lest it hang morosely as an afterthought. The quills, engineered of folded organdy stiffened with wires, modified the gait and complicated the use of the hands. Great difficulty was encountered in scenes of excitement and activity. The other animals were free to scamper to and fro furiously. The porcupine had to demonstrate the same frenzy, but he was unable to make quick, darting movements and was continually confined to a flop-roll-flop-flop-roll scurrying. The quilly serenity of the porcupine could be easily understood when some of the other animals made the mistake of slapping him on his quills; his psychic prominence became expansive when his giant headdress was agitated. The transformation of man into porcupine was completed by the make-up which completely disguised my features. It was no longer I who did it, but the porcupine dwelling within me.

"Existence with the miser and the porcupine was short-lived, but for nearly ten years I have had the uncanny experience of watching myself become a mosaic with regularity. I must have painted my face in the now famous mosaic design of *The Book of Job* 800 times, and each time is a new adventure in the psychology of acting. The art of *applying* the make-up can be basic to characterization. To sit before a mirror and wonder at the naked face is to stare at a segment of our own reality. To begin to paint the design onto the face, ignoring the facial contours, is the initial step in forgetting self and beginning to realize the truth of the character, which must always be larger than ourselves. To watch the familiar features disappear, to be a spectator at a new creature's birth, and, finally, to see the image of the character fully made up and clothed in garments created specifically for it, ideally results in a new humility, and more than that, in a new attempt to materialize the character and to express it more fully in unselfish terms. And what is true for *Job* is true for the other plays as well.

Hal Proske as
Brun the bear

138   139

"What can I say in conclusion? That to animate these creations is easy? Never! But is acting ever easy? That by her imaginative concepts Mrs. Corey takes the creativity out of acting and makes a puppet of the actor? Certainly not! I can only profess that through her designs, she creates an environment for creativity which has been so valuable to my acting that I have difficulty in visualizing how artists can make things of beauty without such assistance. Irene Corey blasts holes in the bulwarks of shallow, unimaginative thinking and helps actors to new theatrical concepts."

. . .

Hal Proske has played the title role in the Everyman Players' productions of *Romans by St. Paul* and *The Book of Job*. He appears in many guises in this book, and here reflects on three of these characters.

"There were simultaneous tryouts for Arthur Fauquez' *Reynard the Fox* and Christopher Fry's *A Sleep of Prisoners*. I wanted to be a poetic soldier. I was cast as a bear. Purposeful observation of any animal, with an eye to selection of detail for translation into character and movement, can be surprising. Still smarting about the poetic soldier, I found little that was surprising at the end of an afternoon with the bears in the Houston Zoo. I looked ruefully at my nearly empty note

pad: 'Small eyes of small value.' 'Bear rolling around playfully.' 'Bears pacing in anger.' 'Bear's hindquarters operate independently of his headquarters.'

"That final observation was my key to the bear's basic mime. Hips roll and surge into the mass of the stomach as the hind legs push and thrust to move the bear forward. Such motion is absorbed by the tremendous belly, and hardly communicates at all with the shoulders. Each limb bends at every joint with all efforts to move or to stop. The hindquarters tend to be carried along by their own momentum after the front of the beast has halted. And consider a bear in flight: he is a **freight train derailed, a runaway cannon, with every member of his body flying in a direction other than that of his headlong plunge.**

"So it went: arms akimbo, body heaving and rolling—in grumbling frustration, in pained hunger, in gleeful pursuit of honey or revenge, in gluttonous stupor, in bearish playfulness. All assured me that, 'By George, I have it!'

"But I had failed to note my strongest impression of the bears—the admirable life force which surges within these creatures. I failed to name it at the time, failed to note it consciously, but once the mechanics of movement were in hand, the memory of the creature's unique vitality informed the whole effort with a vengeance.

140 Hal Proske as St. Paul

"The final element was the gift of the designer: the costume-make-up mask. My eyebrows were gone. The bridge of my nose spread from cheek to cheek. My eyes were reduced to two small circles of black, always peering out from under raised lids, vaguely surprised, hinting at a glimmer of animal cunning. A real sense of size came after I had encased my body in the designer's bear. The pillow-paunch for the early rehearsals was replaced by the real version, which was more than doubled in size. My arms and legs were 30 to 40 inches around, and my skull casing had assumed genuinely ursine proportions. Only a bit of my face peered out from the mass of the new body, and that was no face of mine at all.

"The day-to-day me, already sweltering, was imprisoned in a custom-made, portable steam bath; but the burgeoning bear within came slowly to realize that he was free—free to belch in the hall, free to blunder into the director's office, free to terrify coeds in the shop. One cannot reproach a *bear* for such behaviour and there is no possibility of physical retribution. The actor within was protected from physical and emotional attack by the size and density of his outer self. Brun rushed into the forest on the stage and possessed it. He was finally free to be a bear. He was a bear, like all others, who did not need to question the fact of his existence or his appetite, nor doubt that he had ample power and just sufficient intel-

ligence to satisfy the latter. Of course, there were cowing things like the lion's greater power, or pests like Reynard and his tricks, or dreadful things such as men and dogs, but to Brun they were terrors not to be considered when absent.

"Brun had taken possession of the forest and of the actor somewhere deep within him who had forgotten all about the poetic soldier he wanted to play. (That actor played the soldier six weeks later anyway, but that is another story).

"*Romans by St. Paul* means far too much to me to offer anything like a complete statement here. For it is as much a landmark in the history of my self-discovery as was the role of Brun— surely an expression of one of my more dynamic alter-egos. So I lop off a limb of my own being and offer a piece of it for examination.

"Let us consider three elements of costume which fascinate: one, the cape, which fascinates me; two, the gloves which fascinate Mrs. Corey; and three, the shoes, which fascinate everybody.

"When Paul's great cape settles on my shoulders, none of the significance of the burden is lost on me. I feel the heavy injunction that was on the Apostle to preach and convince, just as surely as I feel the weight of my responsibilities toward the production in performance. I am also aware of a responsibility for making the cape behave itself.

Electra 141

It is a vital extension of my saintly body. In a sustained crossing it may gather air in its great weighted folds, and float majestically behind; but hands of stone and wood are forever reaching out and clutching at it. When the cape has developed momentum, it must be guided so that it will not interfere with the next move. Carpeting underfoot will make it wrap around my body in a turn, or drag ponderously behind every movement, frequently blocking someone else's route. On a stone floor, the cape will come rushing up about my feet and sweep under my heels before I have a chance to set it firmly down.

"Mrs. Corey has expressed her fascination with the long-fingered gloves, for she often sees them as they are donned. Offstage they cripple the actor for all practical manual functions, and the fingers seem to be grotesquely disjointed as the actors fumble with a forgotten piece of paraphernalia, or with a doorknob. On stage, however, they are in harmony with the proceedings, and through careful selection and attention, may acquire a powerful and sensitive vocabulary of expression.

"There is one compelling physical imperative in this production which fascinates everybody: the 'exalted footwear.' A mother may boast, 'It's not as bad as having babies,' but a veteran of *Romans* will always remind you, 'You ought to try it in *Romans*' shoes!' In fact the buskins are about as difficult to master as riding a bicycle, and, considered with the rest of the production, provide the actor a vertical advantage. A carefully measured pace is necessary and contributes to a stately and dignified carriage.

"But talk of elevated shoes, extended fingers, and elaborate capes, can quickly become irrelevant, because it is the actor's job to subordinate them to the total achievement. The cape must obey. The hands must live. The shoes must be invisible. It has been done.

"*Electra* was for me a consummation rather than a revelation. Coming as it did at the end of my undergraduate career, I was able to appreciate the production on many levels—its statement, its language, its primitive yet highly sophisticated power, its passion, its perception of human values, and, above all, its style of visualization, of movement and choric dance, and vocal presentation.

"Here I would like to witness to the very sensible influence on the actors of the physical envelope of space created for the tragedy. The great net of doom hung above, all-pervading. All the surfaces, land and sky, were in lifeless stone gray. Perspective lines raced up the massive, triangular rake, toward their vanishing point in infinity, where fate is ordained and divine mysteries are resolved. The lines drew the eye and the mind of

Hal Proske as
142 the Tutor (left)

both actor and spectator from the altar of Apollo, sole bright symbol of hope and justice, past the dreaded gates of Agamemnon's palace—gates which periodically disgorged its demented inhabitants, malicious or pitiable, each by turn to dominate the chorus or to challenge Electra. The performers celebrated the tragedy of Electra with the conviction and urgency born not of decades of living, nor even of classroom lecture, but rather of a genuine emotional response to physical elements in their environment.

"The Pedagogus, the old tutor, embodies a complex symbolism of life force and of a morality which Sophocles believed to be natural and mandatory. He is ancient—a problem for any actor in his early twenties. He is extremely knowledgeable. With the conviction of divine ordination, he deals as falsely with his enemies as they deal with the world. He understands, as Orestes never will, the nature of the moral corruption that has plagued Argos for nearly two generations. He understands, as Orestes even in his subsequent agonies never will, the whole nature of the crime they are about to avenge. But Sophocles does not deal with Orestes. He ends the play with the chorus's triumphal shout '. . . And this day's work is well done!' So one must assume that the tutor is a very genuine symbol of the desecrated morality which he must see restored before he dies.

"The costume itself offered no physical imperatives comparable to the bear's paunch or the saint's elevated footwear. I noted the tree symbolism. I was able to determine a rhythm in early acting designs with the help of the walking staff. During the two-and-a half hour make-up period I can recall that the intricate twists, curve-and-reverse-curve of the make-up mask, by their subtlety and complexity, helped to deepen my emotional involvement. I recall more vividly watching my fellow actor torturously assume the visage of my enemy, Aegisthus. Covered with the white of hyprocrisy, he slowly adorned himself with the marks and lines of cruelty, lust, and cowardice. He wore them like jewels, with incredible pride, in scorn of the doom he had called upon his own head. Against this enemy, and against his equally depraved consort, Clytemnestra, the old man had to direct the innocent, straightforward youths, Orestes and Pylades, in order to fulfill his promise to the Delphic oracles and to the now mad Electra.

"There are old men with missions. Perhaps they hold in their minds the violently contrasting faces of uncomplicated youth and incredible corruption, as they proceed with desperate persistence to direct the energies of one against the other. Such an impulse was certainly an important motivation for my Pedagogus."

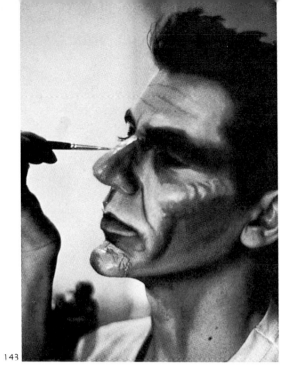

143

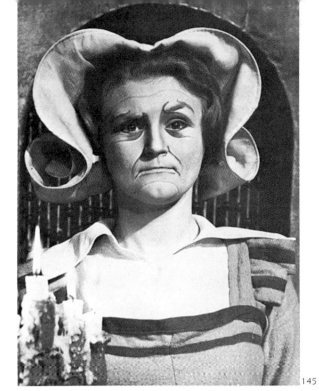

145

Application of traditional stage make-up is covered by several competent authorities. They thoroughly detail realistic modeling by means of shading or dimensional build-up. Lincoln, in Norman Corwin's *The Rivalry*, illustrates the use of these principles.

I would like briefly to examine stylized make-up as it grows out of natural modeling. The stylized face is divided into definite patterns of light and dark to indicate form, rather than relying on gradual shading.

Gines, in *Don Quixote of la Mancha*, serves as an example of this method. As the scarfaced galley slave who was released by Quixote, all lines lead toward his crafty eyes.

Quixote's housekeeper, Dona Belisa, is a softer example, with the major character delineation concentrated around the eyes and mouth.

The make-up chart for Electra emphasizes the bone structure of the face. The accented forehead sets off her deep-set eyes. Orestes (p. 56) and the tutor (p. 62-63) also illustrate stylized realism.

Patterned simplification carries the unique characteristics of the face across a longer distance, contributing to a clearer, and more revealing visage.

144

146

Stylized realism is also used to create an animal make-up mask. The actual animal is studied and dominant features are selected. These are superimposed upon the face of the actor. In some cases the width of the nose is pushed to the edge of the tear ducts, as with the tortoise, wolf, and rabbit. Eyes are

EYES:

Lion   Rabbit

NOSES:

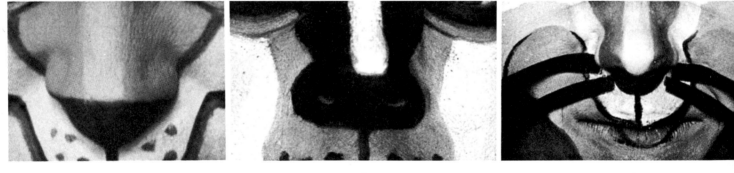

Fox   Badger   Rat

MOUTHS:

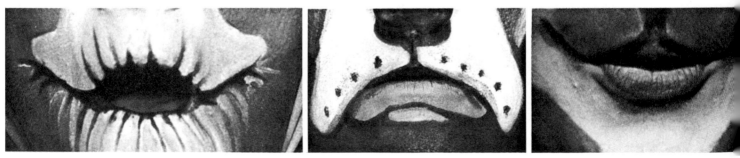

Tortoise   Dog   Marmot

lanted, rounded, enlarged or made wistful. Noses are sharpened, modeled, pointed, widened or pugged. Mouths may wrinkle, droop, grin, become toothy, and smile across the face. The following illustrations demonstrate these differences in eyes, noses and mouths.

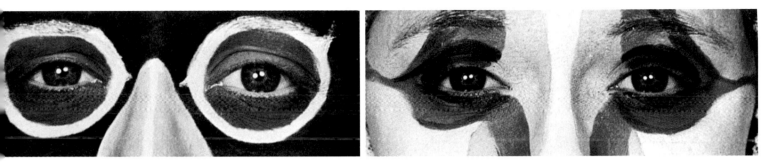

Rook   Hedgehog

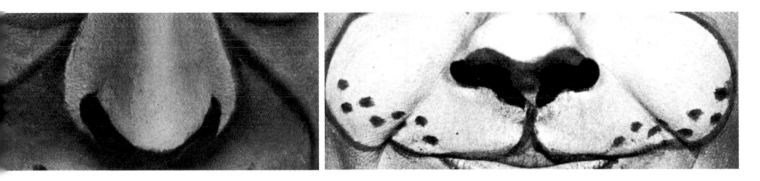

Lion   Rabbit

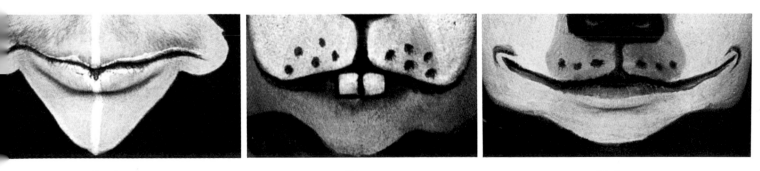

Rook   Hare   Badger

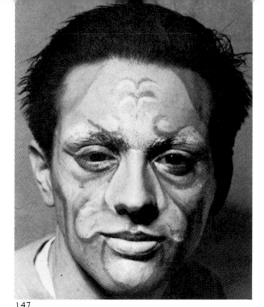

147

Basic areas of lion make-up are outlined or blended before the addition of dark lines.

149

The marmot face grows out of a series of flat unshaded areas of color.

To create a make-up mask with grease paint, one may brush on the major outlines of the face with a medium tone. The position of lines and areas are established in relation to the features of the actor. Then the lightest colors are applied, beginning with the white of the eye. Heavy brown and black accents are added last. Plain white (or flesh-toned) talcum powder sets the grease without dulling the color intensity. Eyes can be retouched after powdering with liquid make-up for extra sharp contrast. In all cases, make-up colors are matched with the costume, so that the eye flows from skin to fabric without break.

Following are typical layout charts for animal make-up.

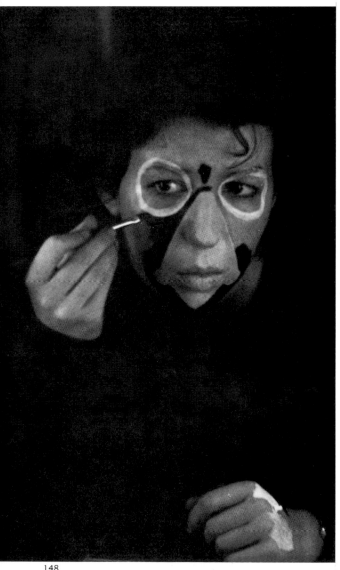

148

Greasepaint is used to create the crow make-up. It is applied with a soft square brush.

MAKE-UP FOR TIECELIN, A CROW *

Make-Up Supplies

Stein's Grease Stick:
No. 25 Black
No. 22 White

Moist Rouge:
No. 3 Medium Red

Liquid Black tooth wax

Optional: Liquid Red

Alcohol: to remove tooth wax

CROW MAKEUP PROCEDURE

1. Draw in all features with #25 Black.
2. Fill in white around the eyes, (Areas A.)
3. Apply Yellow solidly on the beak area, (Area F.)
4. Fill in rest of face solid black. Draw black line of beak over mouth, with the point of the beak being formed on the lower lip.
5. Make thin red lines around the corners of the mouth and around eyes.
6. Draw a white line down the center of the beak, top and bottom.
7. Outline the mouth line in white.

Note: There are no fused lines in this makeup; each area forms a sharp edge against the next one.

*Reprinted from *Reynard the Fox*, by Arthur Fauquez, Anchorage Press, Anchorage, Kentucky.

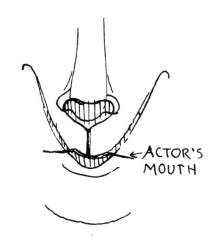

151

Make-Up Supplies

Stein's Grease Stick:
  No. 8 Dark Sunburn
  No. 22 White
  No. 25 Black

Stein's Liner Stick:
  No. 4 Gray
  No. 25 Red-Brown
  No. 16 Yellow

Moist Rouge:
  No. 2 Medium

Mix

Orange
Light Yellow-Orange

Procedure:

1. Orange mixed with Red-Brown; outline all areas and lines.
2. White: Areas A, B, C.
3. Orange: Area E and forehead fading down into Area I; and in Area J.
4. Gray: Area D; shadow under mouth line.
5. Red Brown: Area E, F, G. Fused shadow lines on worry wrinkles in forehead, frown lines, and sides of nose.
6. Light Yellow-Orange: Area H and I. Apply solidly next to nose tip and slanted eye lines, fading toward the top. Area K, fade down from line outward.
7. Black: pupils, brow line, nose, chops, mouth. Dots in Area K and B.
8. Red: Underneath black mouth line.

*Reprinted from *Reynard the Fox* by Arthur Fauquez. Anchorage Press, Anchorage, Ky.

90

MAKE-UP FOR MR. FLEET, A HARE *

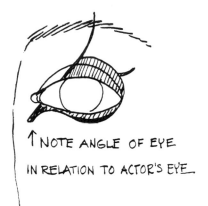

↑ NOTE ANGLE OF EYE
IN RELATION TO ACTOR'S EYE

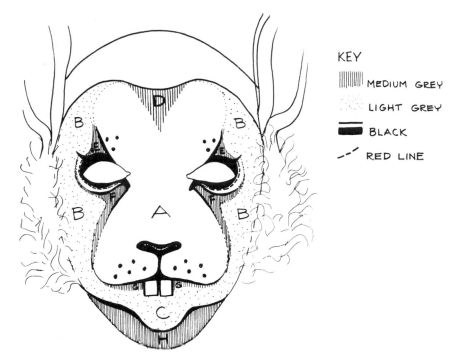

KEY

|||||| MEDIUM GREY

⋮⋮⋮⋮ LIGHT GREY

▬▬ BLACK

⌐ ⌐ RED LINE

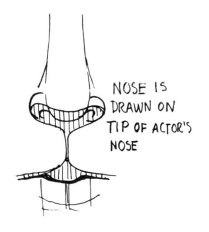

NOSE IS
DRAWN ON
TIP OF ACTOR'S
NOSE

Make-Up Supplies

Stein's Grease Stick:
  No. 22 White

Stein's Liner Stick:
  No. 17 Black

Moist Rouge:
  No. 3 Medium Red

Liquid Black tooth wax

Alcohol: to remove wax

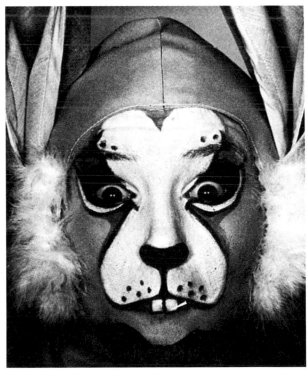

Mix

Light Grey
Medium Grey
Dark Pink

Procedure:

1. Medium Grey: Outline all areas and lines.

2. White: Area A and teeth. Bags under eyes.

3. Light Grey: Areas B, C.

4. Medium Grey: Areas D, E, F, G, H.

5. Black: Pupils, lines above and below eyes, chops, teeth, chin.

6. Red: Along black pupils above white bag under eyes. Inner corner of eye.

7. For best effect of painted teeth, black out teeth with liquid black tooth wax.

*Reprinted from *The Great Cross-Country Race* by Alan Broadhurst. Anchorage Press, Anchorage, Ky.

KEY

▦	AREA #25 RED-BROWN
▥	LINE #25 RED-BROWN
⠿	HIGHLIGHT {BEIGE or WHITE}
▨	LIGHT RED-BROWN
▬	BLACK LINE
⬛	BLACK AREA
- - -	RED LINE
▦	MEDIUM RED BROWN

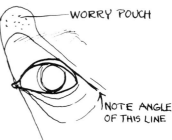

WORRY POUCH

NOTE ANGLE OF THIS LINE

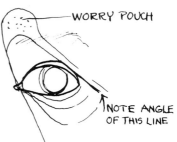

NOSE, DRAWN HALF WAY ON NOSTRIL AROUND TIP AND UNDER

Make-Up Supplies

Stein's Grease Stick:
  No. 8 Dark Sunburn
  No. 22 White
  No. 5L Ivory Yellow

Stein's Liner Stick:
  No. 17 Black
  No. 25 Red-Brown

Moist Rouge:
  No. 3 Medium Red

153

Mix

Medium Reddish Brown.
Light Reddish Brown.
Beige color. (Lighter than the light Reddish Brown, yet darker than White.)

Procedure:

1. Using Medium Brown, outline all areas, eyes, bags under the eyes, but NOT forehead wrinkles.

2. White: fill in Area A.

3. Pale Beige: Areas B, C.

4. Light Red Brown: Areas D, E, F.

5. Medium Red Brown: Areas G, H.

6. No. 25 Red Brown: Areas J, K, L, M, N. Also shadowed dip in forehead.

7. No. 25 Brown: Line forehead wrinkles, shadow along mouth (along bottom of Area A) and top of Area G.

8. Pale Beige Highlight: Worry pouches above lines, between worry lines on forehead, cheek bones.

9. Light Red Brown: Spots, freckles, muzzle (Areas A and B).

10. Black: Eyes, eyebrows, side of nose, cheeks, mouth, chin, nose.

11. Red: Lips, a line below mouthline.

*Reprinted from *The Great Cross-Country Race* by Alan Broadhurst. Anchorage Press, Anchorage, Ky.

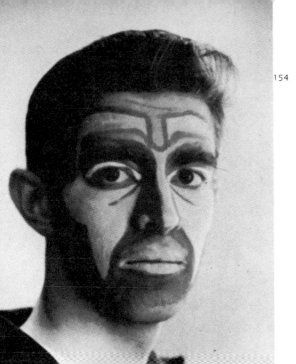

154

Make-up for St. Paul, showing the basic areas laid in with liquid make-up.

The black accent lines are added to make-up.

155

Completed make-up for St. Paul with wig and beard added. A fake forehead elongates the face.

156

Where area blending is not desired, liquid make-up may be used for the make-up mask. It is painted directly onto the skin with flat red sable brushes. Liquid application is faster than greasepaint. In *Romans by St. Paul* the eyes are moved upward in the face because of the elongation of the forehead. The pupil is painted on the lid of the natural eye. Shadows and skin tones are laid in first, then the features are outlined in black. The sculptural effect is realized with the addition of the wig and beard.

Make-up for a member of the women's chorus in *The Book of Job* begins with the painting of the enlarged eyes and 157 pupils, and the nose-brow lines.

Mosaic squares of liquid make-up fol158 low the contour of the face.

Make-up chart for *Job* mosaic make-up.
159

In the mosaic make-up for *The Book of Job*, the eyes are outlined first with half-pupils painted beneath the actor's eyes and continued on the lid. All other features are then made in relation to these "false" eyes, with strong emphasis on the brow, nose, mouth, and chin. The mosaic pattern, painted in narrower black lines, follows the contour of the face. The squares are filled with peach, pink (for intermediate shadows), and green (for deeper shadows). White around the pupils defines the eyes. Red at the tear ducts and lips adds vitality.

94

In my desire to illustrate the indivisibility of costumes and make-up, I have chosen dramatic examples, feeling that the more common realizations would be less useful. However, whether the play is realistic or not, the same rules of unity apply.

Indeed, the principles involving the union of make-up and costume apply to ballet and opera, also. Although ballet has arrived at certain stereotypes in its classic tradition, it constantly seeks to reflect tempos of the modern scene. The old as well as the new can be evaluated in terms of visual expression of the internal content of the music. The convention of stressing only eye make-up on the dancers could be elaborated to emphasize the rest of the face, as has already evolved in the older dance forms of the Kathakali or the Peking Opera. Perhaps it is because ballet is relatively new as compared with the ancient court dance of the Bugaku and the Noh of Japan, or the Khon and Lakhon of Thailand, that it has not yet merged movement and visual form into one entity.

The search for images with which to enhance the actor or the singer or the dancer is a difficult one. Any creative expression calls for a marshalling of all forces to forge toward a new idea. I have always felt extreme empathy for the tormented creature in the Steig cartoon who is clinging to and inching up the steep sides of a mountain toward the peak, gasping, "I can't quite express it!" We, too, never quite express it, but the gain is all in the trying.

Oberon, addressing Puck, describes a little Western flower he once saw struck by Cupid's flaming shaft. "Fetch me that flower!" he commands. Puck does not whine, "But I'm not sure I can find it." Nor does he buy one at the florist's to save himself a trip, or substitute one he happens to have on hand, or pick a common flower near by. It may take us longer than forty minutes, but let us be as bold as Puck and *girdle the globe* in our effort to bring back the perfect blossom with all its mysterious power intact. Knowing that Oberon will know the true from the false, let us respond to his order, "Fetch me *that* flower!"

Oberon in *A Midsummer Night's Dream.*

160

5

The Imaginative Theatre

"Formulae entail a certain rigidity and fixity,
and anything that freezes is anti-theatre. . . the
art of the theatre is the art of life, and life is
the contrary of rigidity and fixity; it is on
the contrary something moving, complex and
varied, and it can't be enclosed in any formula."

Jean-Louis Barrault
*The Theatre of Jean-Louis
Barrault*

:k plucks the magic flower in *A
dsummer Night's Dream.*

THE imaginative theatre begins in a confrontation with the abstract. Returning to search the mask for its source of inner strength, we see again that terrible vitality. Joseph Gregor refers to it as a world phenomenon exempt from time and space. "Poised on the mask are all the terrible experiences and fancies of mankind. . . Here in our hand we hold one of the most effective keys to the secret realm of our own past."

I wonder if there is significant difference between the fears and terrors mirrored there and those experienced today in our age of space conquering and time killing. Having controlled our material elements, we have left the space of the mind largely unexplored.

Jean-Louis Barrault observes that the mask at one and the same time can partake of the visible and the invisible. We must not necessarily be literal and mask all our players, but to penetrate the abstract and comprehend its power will enable us to create a more evocative theatre.

The mask is but a forerunner in the continuing attempt of the artist to forge a shape for the Gods. To invest wood and stone with a hidden mystique, is to create what André Malraux calls "the power that certain figures have of impregnating space with the divine." "When we contemplate them, when we overhear their silent dialogue . . . we make the . . . discovery . . . that for thousands of years the major aim of all artistic creation was to reveal or to uphold forms of truth." This too, is the goal of the theatre.

Hilton Edwards refers to art as a bridge that allows us to cross time and space, enabling us to visit a world beyond our normal comprehension.

162
A real bassett encounters the mystery of the mask.

It is the artist who has grappled with the infinite, focusing it to our vision. His is the task of eliminating chaos, and ordering the underlying forms into a vital sub-structure. This submerged order of art creates the forms which come to the surface. Anton Ehrenzweig, in his book *The Hidden Order of Art*, explores the theory that our frequent misapprehension of the artist lies in our desire to cling to known, conscious forms of order, fearfully rejecting his new manifestations. Art which does not disrupt becomes sterile in its acceptance. The imaginative theatre will constantly strive to find new forms, ever mindful that it is the complex structure underneath, reinforced by underlying research, that molds the visible shape.

What big eyes a designer needs! How can he ever see enough? Mark Van Doren says: "What we call creation is nothing but noticing—and then, of course, reflecting and rendering what has been noticed. But first of all noticed." Seeing and perceiving, the artist must make relations, ordering all into a single design. In the same way that the inventive Leonardo da Vinci wandered through his native Italy observing the flow of water, the placement of a shell, the flight of a bird—so must we discover our surroundings.

What clear vision, what long-distance focus a designer needs! For if he loses sight of the goal, how can he ever reach his destination? Side trips are fascinating, but diverting. Mutations at any one point may throw the whole organism out of balance.

Autolycus in *The Winters' Tale* sees the world through his baubles and trinkets.

163

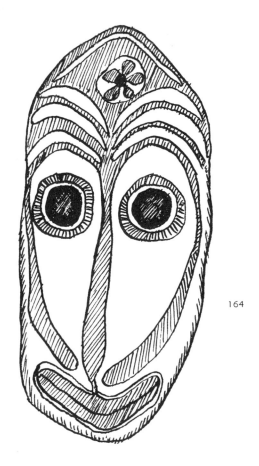

164

With a motley burst of color Petruchio arrives to claim his bride, accompanied by his lackey, Grumio, in *The Taming of* 165 *the Shrew*.

Nor are these characteristics any less applicable to the other artists of the theatre, especially the director and the playwright. These leaders are responsible for weaving the specialized talents of other artists into the fabric of the whole theatre. It was Leonardo who realized that the composition of the picture is the greatest of its parts. The "whole" perspective allows the actor to relate to something larger than his own ego. The imaginative theatre strives to be a unified theatre.

Gestation in design cannot be rushed. If it is, the result may be a premature birth or, tragically,

the idea may be still-born. I experienced this danger in a production of *The Taming of the Shrew*, when designing was pressured into a short period. The induction scene was color-keyed in shades of red, maroon and pink, and was staged on the left front apron. Brightly clad troubadors carted, carried, and erected their black and white setting on a raked stage, painted in a parquet of black and white. Production based on these designs continued through dress rehearsal week.

At the midnight end of the final rehearsal, a belated idea of mine surfaced and refused to go away. Since the staging was black and white, then the induction should be black and white also! To this neutral world the traveling troupe should bring a colorful explosion of farce. Was there time to change nine costumes and the set pieces in the twenty hours before opening? The understanding director said only, "The idea is right. It's up to you, I'll help you." We took the fatal plunge. The couch was recovered, the props repainted. Costumes were machine dyed (too light), dye boiled (shrank), dried (still too light) —then sprayed with black enamel or made over completely. Warm from the ironing board, they were handed over to astonished actors by an exhausted crew, who dubbed the ordeal, "The Day the World Turned Black and White." Was it worth it? Yes! The design before had been hurried into adequacy, but was not exceptional. Only at the last moment did the idea join the thoughts which had gone before to create a simple jeweler's setting for the multicolored play within the play.

Setting for *The Taming of the Shrew*, with costumes for the induction scene executed in black and white.

Heavy walls and strong side lighting create a sculptural plasticity in the setting for Lorca's *Yerma.*
167

Just as there are varying periods of gestation in the animal world, there is no set time for birthing a design. The amount of experience available to feed it will affect its formation. New ideas which were tapped but not fully explored in previous plays, may furnish impetus. Or the research may provide new material for assimilation. Ideas can appear in an instant with the glow of a meteor, but they are only valid if they shed light on the play at hand. To catch at the sparks before the flame appears is to grasp for instant inspiration, leaving the play unignited.

A visiting European art teacher was criticized at the end of one year for the seeming lack of facility by his students. He remarked, "Even in America, Minute Rice takes five minutes."

Given the power of observation and perception, the designer needs two other qualities which can be cultivated but not caught: curiosity and imagination. Travel is perhaps the greatest stimulus; exposure and horizon-stretching the by-products. Since one can travel by book as well as boat, there is no excuse.

What should be the areas of formal study? How could the list be limited? Strange, unexpected, half-forgotten bits of one's life crop up for use in the most exciting way. All experience and knowledge is eventually utilized. If you don't have it, you certainly can't use it! Mark Van Doren states that the more doctors, divines and statesmen know about everything, the more effective they will be. The same applies to artists. "They do not start from scratch; they start by scratching—by peering, by digging, by diving, and coming up again."

Yet there are certain areas of training that are more helpful than others. Most useful of all is a familiarity with the arts. The designer should know the effects of volume and texture, how to reflect a period in furniture and furnishings, how to get impact from color; he should be aware of the revelation through line, and the emergence of mood through light and shadow. Sculpture, architecture, painting, and interior decoration can be modified into meaningful theatrical design. These art forms meet on the stage and there unite, enhanced by their new theatrical relationship. But they must be transformed to new service.

In a mechanized world where crafts are relegated to side show entertainment in museums and tourist centers, the art of the hand becomes ever more rare. In the midst of our dependence on and respect for machines, the miracle of the hand comes as a surprise. Since we do not experience the making of the product by our own hand and effort, the result is a loss of pride in work. Because we all tend to be mere parts of vast machinery oriented toward some institutional end, we seldom ever experience the personal joy of seeing a work started and carried through from seed to fruition.

In an era of regulated hours, guaranteed salaries, and fringe benefits, more attention is given to featherbedding than to how the bed is made—or, in the long look, who is going to lie in it. It is my suspicion that Pride-in-Work lies there, with a gilded lily in its hand. A theatre without craftsmanship becomes a gimmicked mockery or a sloppy morass.

There has always been and will continue to be a need for skilled, proud craftsmen in the theatre. Whatever the training, whether via the colleges, or by experience, craft must not be ignored.

Katherine, in Shakespeare's *Henry V*, utilizes the elegance of the gothic line.
168

To be an efficient painter and draftsman is imminently useful. Knowledge of methods of construction and lighting makes for coherent design. Yet skill in these areas alone will not supplant that prime ingredient—imagination. Respect for and knowledge of materials strengthen the designer. However, there is danger in being so enamored of materials and their effect that the purpose for their use is forgotten. Many a marriage between visual concept and play spirit has been ruined by the designer's affair with a material.

The theatre is not a showplace for the artist's talents. But he can serve as a catalyst between the meaning of the play and the perception of the audience.

The setting of *Under Milkwood* evoked a hill of windows leading down to the sea. Townspeople bustled up and down tri-level streets; the "drowned" rose up from the sea. At night villagers "slept" vertically with covers pulled up to their chins as spots moved from dream to dream.
169

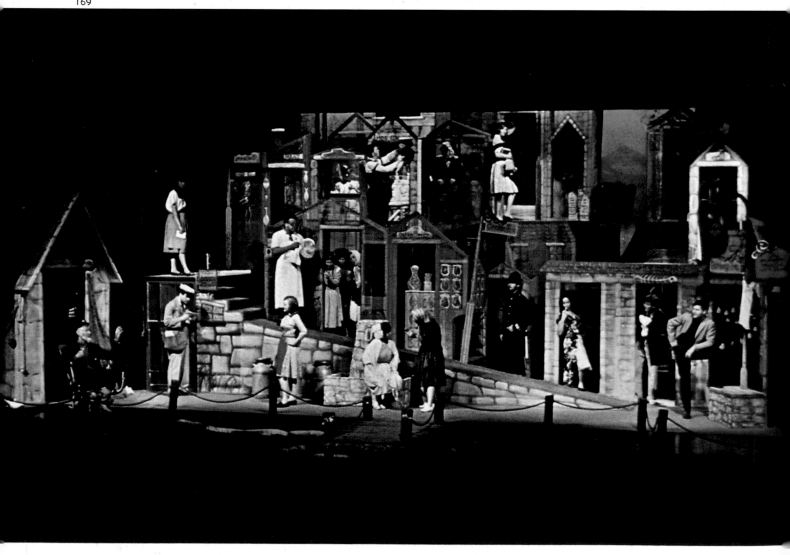

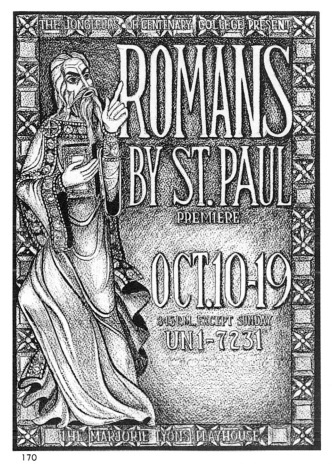
170

171

Posters which carry out the design concept of production, further strengthening unity of design.

Yet still the question: How does one become a theatre craftsman? There is no known formula. To learn all the *tricks* of perspective will not guarantee perspective on the theatre. Perhaps more crucial is attitude. One must learn to eliminate the phrase, "It will do," and replace it with, *"Is it right?"* Such an attitude toward the work will create high standards. Although perfection may be unattainable, it is a better goal than "getting by."

One of the gratifying mysteries of mankind is the appearance of that many-splendored attribute known as "talent." The source of its glow is untraced, an evanescent gift of the gods. Yet, in all its compelling allure, it is of such fragile nature

that it cannot long stand without reinforcement. Call this armature will power, call it discipline, or whatever, but above all, call it essential. For eons lightning snapped and cracked with jagged restlessness until it was harnessed into "electricity." Channeled force assumes meaning. The theatre needs talent; talent which is directed, motivated, challenged.

I long ago lost track of the number of idle-eyed spectators who, leaning against the table where my brush stroked furiously against the canvas and against the clock, say, "How I envy you your talent." It is then that my weary bones cry out, "Why don't you envy me my discipline?"

172
An audience at an inn, fascinated by a traveling puppet show in *Don Quixote of la Mancha*.

High standards demand an honest solution, not an easy one. When studying with the French artist Reynold Arnould, I asked how I would manage when I no longer had his criticism to guide me. He replied, "Just say whatever you have to say, *the hardest way you can say it*." Great images are not born of small effort. They cost a great price. They have lasting value.

Another elusive mystery is taste. When so many decisions and selections are involved in visualizing a play, they are bound to be a reflection of the taste of the artist. But what is taste? Could it be said to be the result of a series of decisions based upon past experience? If so, the wider the *perceptive* experience or exposure, the better the

taste will be. In selecting some details, one is also eliminating others, and it is just as important to know what to leave out. The Japanese have a word, *Shibui*, meaning that a thing has been reduced to its simplest element. Good taste is found in this kind of understatement.

Is the imaginative theatre in any way discouraged by the realities of box office? I think not. In the theatre a price tag is not a true measure of the product. Producers are still lacing up their boots with ideas launched by Joan Littlewood in her "shoestring" Theatre Workshop in London over a decade ago. Our original *Job* production was staged for less than $100.00. We have always followed the policy of never looking down on the appreciative capacity of our audience, or the capability of our actors. We strive to present the best we can produce, and to produce the best we can imagine. We find that they respond to the challenge. Television has lifted the responses of the public, although more by sating them with the banal than by presenting them with drama of dimension.

Of course, educational theatre does not have the financial headaches of Broadway. In a sense, the colleges and universities serve as "patrons" of the theatre, "underwriting" by means of staff salaries and buildings. This has contributed to the decentralization of theatre in America. There is more freedom for experimentation. Yet, lest it be assumed that educational theatre exists totally in a bed of ivy-leaved roses, consider some of the thorns. There is the prick of jealousy that stirs the recumbent academic when recognition of the work of the theatre "threatens" his niche of security. There are the frequent administrative directives sent to prune the bush, lest the blossoms become the envy of some less productive department. The very opulence of the facilities sometimes arouses academic suspicions, bringing into question artistic achievement. Even in intellectual circles, the tendency is to prefer diversion rather than stimulation, formula rather than experimentation. Whatever frustrations evolve from people structured in a working relationship either in the professional theatre, or any other work, the same frustrations are present where the college acts as "patron."

Difficulties, however, should not be allowed to prevent the presentation of truth in our theatres. The need is too urgent. In theatre we hope to

173

Major Barbara, Act III, of the George Bernard Shaw comedy.

see ethical delineation and character revelation—a guide for living. Civilization is a fragile plant which comes with no guarantee for its survival. It is easily encroached upon by the jungle of ignorance. This week there are a million more people in the world than last week. Several times a second a spank-and-wail heralds the arrival of another "barbarian", and civilization is again in jeopardy as we face the challenge of teaching him all we know and guiding him toward what he must find out for himself. Our theatre should be a "pleasant teacher," the ideal place to create an atmosphere where great language is heard, where the universal is evoked, where truth is revealed.

There is no success formula. "All rules have no other value than as corroboration of created form. . . For if you were to use rules in creating, you would never get to the beginning of anything, and your work would be confused." Again, Leonardo da Vinci, that ancient seer, leads our way.

This brave theatre of ours will accept limitations —be it budget, corset, or mask—as a challenge. Working within the confines set up by these restrictions, we shall find new solutions, create new departures. What is wrong with a theatre of poverty, if it is rich in imagination? Why not elaborate theatre as long as it is not gilt over wormy wood, or embroidery on rotten cloth? Whatever the situation, whatever the limitation, we must conjure with imagination and execute with intuition.

And on the way, don't forget to break the rules.

Tortoise and hare at the finish line in *The Great Cross-Country Race*.
174

CREDITS

Photographer

   JERRY MITCHELL*

Director

   ORLIN COREY*

Designer

   IRENE COREY

Producing Groups

   THE EVERYMAN PLAYERS

   A professional company based in Pineville, Kentucky
   Produced by Orlin and Irene Corey

   THE JONGLEURS OF CENTENARY COLLEGE

   Shreveport, Louisiana

   THE MASKRAFTERS OF GEORGETOWN COLLEGE

   Georgetown, Kentucky

*Exceptions indicated under Illustration Data

SOURCE-BOOKS QUOTED

Andre Malraux, *The Metamorphosis of the Gods*, Doubleday & Co., New York.

William Fagg and Margaret Plass, *Primitive Art*, Dutton Vista Picturebook, London.

Carl Frederick Engelstad, "The Norsemen", Vol. XIV, No. 3, May-June, 1956.

Richard Southern, *The Seven Ages of Theatre*, Hill and Wang, New York.

Earl Ernst, *The Kabuki Theatre*, Oxford University Press.

Robert Edmund Jones, *The Dramatic Imagination*, Theatre Arts Books, New York.

Gordon Craig, *The Art of the Theatre*, William Heinemann, Ltd., London.

Stark Young, *The Theatre*, Hill and Wang, New York.

Hilton Edwards, *The Mantle of Harlequin*, Progress House, Dublin.

Joseph Gregor, *Masks of the World*, London.

Jean-Louis Barrault, *The Theatre of Jean-Louis Barrault*, Hill and Wang, New York.

Anton Ehrenzweig, *The Hidden Order of Art*, Weidenfeld and Nicolson, London.

Mark Van Doren, *Creative America*, Ridge Press, New York.

ILLUSTRATION DATA

Numerals refer to small numbers beside each illustration

Cover: Hal Proske as Job. Photo, Preston Slusher.

1. Tsimshian Wind Mask. Courtesy of the American Museum of Natural History.

2. Sketch for setting of *Hedda Gabler*. Produced at Georgetown College, 1958.

3. Set design for *The Prisoner*. Produced at Centenary College, 1963.

4. *The Book of Job*. Premiered at Georgetown College, 1957. Don Rutledge photos/Black Star.

5. Gay Farley, Randolph Tallman and Louella Bains in *The Book of Job*, Coventry Cathedral, September 1964. Photo: Richard Sadler.

6. Walter Rhodes as Eliphaz in *The Book of Job*.

7. The Everyman Players in *Romans by St. Paul* at Southwark Cathedral, October 1966. Photo: Keystone Press Agency, Ltd.

8. Costume designs for *The Rivalry*. Produced at Centenary College, 1961.

9. Lorine Crenshaw as Mrs. Douglas.

10. Ibid.

11. Costume and mask design for Chorus, in *The Winter's Tale*. Produced at Centenary College, 1962.

12. *The Crucible*, produced at Centenary College, 1961.

13. Don Farley as Leontes in *The Winter's Tale*.

14. *The Winter's Tale*, ACT I.

15. Warren Hammack as Job in *The Book of Job*.

16. Sketch of mosaic at San Vitale, Ravenna.

17. Everyman Players in *The Book of Job*. Don Rutledge photos/Black Star.

18. Martha Moore, make-up demonstration. Don Rutledge photos/Black Star.

19. Costume and make-up design for the male chorus of *The Book of Job*.

20. Costume and make-up design for the female chorus of *The Book of Job*.

21. Costume and make-up design for Job, in *The Book of Job*.

22. Hal Proske as Job in *The Book of Job*.

23. Everyman Players in *The Book of Job*. Don Rutledge photos/Black Star.

24. Hal Proske as Eliphaz in *The Book of Job*.

25. Costume and make-up design for Electra in Sophocles' *Electra*.

26. Costume and make-up designs for *The Crucible*.

27. Grace Jackson as Elizabeth Proctor in *The Crucible*.

28. Don Quixote as illustrated by Gustave Doré.

29. Allen Shaffer as Don Quixote in *Don Quixote of la Mancha*. Premiered at Centenary College, Nov., 1965.

30. Make-up design for Brando Notcouth in *The Great Cross Country Race*. Produced at Centenary College, 1967.

31. Mickey Fahey as Brando Notcouth. Photo: George Gibbons.

32. Make-up design for Sophia, in *The Great Cross Country Race*.

33. Lauretta Maloney as Sophia Notcouth in *The Great Cross County Race*. Photo: George Gibbons.

34. Make-up design for Maude in *The Great Cross Country Race*.

35. Make-up design for George in *The Great Cross Country Race*.

36. Maureen Buckley as Maude, and David Adams as George in *The Great Cross Country Race*.

37. Mickey Fahey, Douglas Frasier, and Steve Pearce in *The Great God Brown*. Directed by Phillip D. Anderson at Centenary College, 1967. Photo: George Gibbons.

38. John Goodwin as Dion in *The Great God Brown*. Photo: George Gibbons.

39. Paper sculpture mask of Margaret in *The Great God Brown*. Photo: Fred Chapman.

40. Paper sculpture mask of Brown's secretary in *The Great God Brown*. Photo: Fred Chapman.

41. Dion's second mask; paper sculpture, *The Great God Brown*. Photo: Fred Chapman.

42. Jeannie Marlin Smith as the masked Cybele. *The Great God Brown*. Photo: George Gibbons.

43. Study sketch for a fox.

44. Randolph Tallman in the title role of *Reynard the Fox*. Produced at Centenary College, 1962.

45. Study sketch for a porcupine.

46. Bob Harmon as Rev. Epinard, the porcupine, in *Reynard the Fox*.

47. Ibid.

48. Allen Shaffer as Noble the lion in *Reynard the Fox*.

49. Ibid

50. Wiley Cameron as Rev. Epinard the porcupine, and Bo Hatch as Reynard the fox in *Reynard the Fox*. Produced by the Everyman Players at Ken Lake State Park, 1965.

ILLUSTRATION DATA (Continued)

51. Nita Fran Hutchison as Mrs. Warren the rabbit, and Jimmy Journey as Mr. Fleet the hare in *The Great Cross Country Race.*

52. Study sketch for the hare.

53. Study sketch for the rabbit.

54. David Kingsley as Mr. Basket, a hound dog, in *The Great Cross Country Race.*

55. Study sketch for the dog.

56. Charlie Brown as Mr. Sett, a Badger, in *The Great Cross Country Race.*

57. Costume and make-up design for Calaban in *The Tempest.* Produced at Georgetown College, 1957.

58. John Groth as Mr. Paddle, a water rat, in *The Great Cross Country Race.*

59. Ken Holamon as Mr. Sloe, the tortoise, and John Groth as Mr. Paddle, the water rat in *The Great Cross Country Race.*

60. Ken Holamon and Jimmy Journey studying a tortoise at the Houston zoo. Photo: Douglas Frasier.

61. Paulette James as a woodsprite (scene changer) in *Reynard the Fox.* Photo: Constance Stuart.

62. Costume sketch for Mustard Seed in *A Midsummer Night's Dream.*

63. Ruthanne Cozine as Moth in *A Midsummer Night's Dream.* Produced at Centenary College, 1963.

64. Katie O'Mary as Cobweb in *A Midsummer Night's Dream.*

65. Barbara McMillian as Peaseblossom in *A Midsummer Night's Dream.*

66. Study sketch of Vulturine guinea fowl.

67. Costume sketch for Snout the Tinker in *A Midsummer Night's Dream.*

68. Study sketch of a bird of paradise.

69. Costume and make-up design for Titania in *A Midsummer Night's Dream.*

70. Study sketch of a grouse.

71. Costume and make-up design for Oberon in *A Midsummer Night's Dream.*

72. Virginia Bobbit as Titania, and Allen Shaffer as Oberon in *A Midsummer Night's Dream.*

73. Randolph Tallman as Puck in *A Midsummer Night's Dream.*

74. Study sketch of a masked tanager.

75. Randolph Tallman as Puck in *A Midsummer Night's Dream.*

76. Ruthanne Cozine as Tiecelin, a crow, in *Reynard the Fox.*

77. Sculptured figures on the Royal Portal of Chartres Cathedral. Photo: Orlin Corey.

78. Costume and make-up designs for *Romans by St. Paul.*

79. Everyman Players in *Romans by St. Paul.* Premiered at The First Baptist Church, Shreveport, Louisiana, 1963.

80. *The Miser.* Produced at Centenary College, 1961.

81. Sketch of a half-mask for the Commedia dell' Arte character, Pantalone.

82. George Bryan as Harpagon in *The Miser.*

83. Sketch of a Northwest Coast Indian deer mask from the Chicago Museum of Natural History.

84. Russell Johnson (partly obscured), Jimmy Journey and Irene Corey studying horses. Photo: Lloyd Stilley, Shreveport Times.

85. Jimmy Journey inside framework for horse. Photo: John T. Moseley, Shreveport Times.

86. Jimmy Journey as Rosinante, and Allen Shaffer as Don Quixote, in *Don Quixote of la Mancha.*

87. Irene Corey, Jimmy Journey. Photo: John T. Moseley, The Shreveport Times.

88. Jimmy Journey as the spirit of Rosinante, in *Don Quixote of la Mancha.*

89. Costume designs for the workmen in *The Zeal of Thy House.*

90. Costume and make-up design for Michael in *The Zeal of Thy House.*

91. Costume and make-up design for Gabriel in *The Zeal of Thy House.*

92. John Sharp as Gabriel, Paul Davis as Raphael, Bill Clifton as Michael in *The Zeal of Thy House.* Photo: Gene Diskey.

93. Make-up study for the three witches in *Macbeth.* Produced at Georgetown College, 1954.

94. Costume and make-up design for Tempter I, in *Murder in the Cathedral.*

95. Wiley Cameron as Tempter I, in *Murder in the Cathedral.* Produced at Centenary College, 1960.

96. Costume and make-up design for Tempter II, in *Murder in the Cathedral.*

97. Costume and make-up design for Tempter III in *Murder in the Cathedral.*

98. Robert Shy as Tempter IV, in *Murder in the Cathedral.*

99. Ibid.

100. Left to right, (first row): John Williams as Beckett, Ray Chabeau as Tempter III; (second row): Wiley Cameron as Tempter I, James Foster as Tempter II; (back row): Robert Shy as Tempter IV.

101. Setting for *Electra* by Sophocles. Produced at Centenary College, 1964.

102. The sacred horns of Mycenae at the Palace of Knossos in Crete. Photo: Orlin Corey.

103. Electra and women's chorus in *Electra*.

104. Marshall Oglesby as Orestes in *Electra*.

105. Ibid.

106. Costume and make-up design for Chrysothemes in *Electra*.

107. Sandra West as a slave to the queen in *Electra*.

108. Sandra West and Sharon Hubert as slaves to the queen in *Electra*.

109. Costume and make-up design for Aegisthus in *Electra*.

110. Barry Hope as Aegisthus in *Electra*.

111. Make-up chart for Aegisthus.

112. Costume and make-up design for Clytemnestra in *Electra*.

113. Ruthanne Cozine as Clytemnestra in *Electra*.

114. Make-up chart for Clytemnestra.

115. Costume and make-up design for the Tutor in *Electra*.

116. Make-up chart for the Tutor.

117. Hal Proske as the Tutor in *Electra*.

118. Hal Proske as St. Paul in *Romans by St. Paul*.

119. Costume chart for *The Merry Wives of Windsor*. Produced Centenary College.

120. Costume design for King Onion in *The Magic Garden* by Irene Corey. Produced at Georgetown College.

121. Hal Proske as Cleante in *The Miser*.

122. George Bryan as Rev. Epinard, the porcupine, in *Reynard the Fox*. 1964 touring production of the Everyman Players. Photo: Constance Stuart.

123. George Bryan as Eliphaz in *The Book of Job*. Photo: Constance Stuart.

124. John Groth as Mr. Paddle, the water rat in *The Great Cross Country Race*.

125. Louella Bains as a member of the women's chorus in *Romans by St. Paul*.

126. Sylvia Cardwell as Lendore the marmot, in *Reynard the Fox*.

127. Roy Depuys as Brun the bear in *Reynard the Fox*. Everyman Players production at Ken Lake State Park, Kentucky, 1965.

128. Don Humphrey as Ysengrin the wolf in *Reynard the Fox*. Everyman Players production at Ken Lake State Park, Kentucky, 1965.

129. Gene Hay as Mr. Spiney the hedgehog, in *The Great Cross Country Race*.

130. Stained glass window, Chartres Cathedral. Photo: Orlin Corey.

131. Costume and make-up design for the women's chorus in *Murder in the Cathedral*.

132. Women's chorus of *Murder in the Cathedral*, produced at Centenary College.

133. Ken Holamon as Mr. Sloe, the tortoise in *The Great Cross Country Race*.

134. Gay Farley as Tiecelin the crow in *Reynard the Fox*. 1964 Touring Production of the Everyman Players.

135. Costume and make-up design for the Miser in *The Miser*.

136. George Bryan as Rev. Epinard, the porcupine in *Reynard the Fox*. 1964 touring production of the Everyman Players. Photo: Constance Stuart.

137. George Bryan as Eliphaz in *The Book of Job*.

138. Hal Proske as Brun in *Reynard the Fox*.

139. Hal Proske as Brun. 1964 touring production of the Everyman Players. Photo: Constance Stuart.

140. Hal Proske as St. Paul in *Romans by St. Paul*.

141. Barry Hope as Aegisthus, Jim Shull as Pylades, Marshall Oglesby as Orestes in *Electra*.

142. Hal Proske as the Tutor, Marshall Oglesby as Orestes, in *Electra*.

143. Robert Shy applying make-up for the role of Lincoln in *The Rivalry*.

144. David Kingsley as Gines the puppeteer in *Don Quixote of la Mancha*.

145. Dorothy Bradley as Dona Belisa, the housekeeper, in *Don Quixote of la Mancha*.

146. Make-up chart for Electra in *Electra*.

147. Allen Shaffer in first stages of lion make-up for *Reynard the Fox*.

148. Ruthanne Cozine applying make-up for the crow in *Reynard the Fox*.

149. Barbara McMillian applying make-up for the marmot in *Reynard the Fox*. Photo: Constance Stuart.

150. Gay Farley as a crow.

151. Randolph Tallman as a fox.

152. Dorothy Bradley as a hare.

153. Dorothy Bradley as a dog.

154. Hal Proske in intermediary stage of make-up for St. Paul.

155. Hal Proske in final stage of make-up for St. Paul. Don Rutledge photos/Black Star .

156. Hal Proske in completed make-up and costume for St. Paul.

157. Gay Farley applying liquid make-up for the women's chorus in *The Book of Job*.

158. Gay Farley in completed mosaic make-up. Don Rutledge photos/Black Star.

159. Make-up chart for the mosaic make-up used for *The Book of Job*.

160. Allen Shaffer as Oberon in *A Midsummer Night's Dream*.

161. Randolph Tallman as Puck in a *Midsummer Night's Dream*.

162. Paulette James and Pat Bird as hound dogs in *Reynard the Fox*. Photo: The Natal Mercury, Durban, South Africa.

163. Allen Shaffer as Autolycus in *A Winter's Tale*.

164. New Guinea gable end from the Chicago Museum of Natural History.

165. Marshall Oglesby as Grumio, Barry Hope as Petruchio in *The Taming of the Shrew*.

166. Orlin Corey as a Lord, Bonnie Henry as Sly's "wife," and Judy Contonis as the Maid in *The Taming of the Shrew*.

167. Marsha Harper as Yerma in Garcia Lorca's *Yerma*. Directed by Donald Musselman at Centenary College, 1966.

168. Carol Lynn Thomas as Katherine in Henry V. Produced at Centenary College, 1966.

169. *Under Milkwood*, produced at Centenary College, 1967.

170. Poster for *Romans by St. Paul*, designed by Irene Corey.

171. Poster for Ibsen's *Ghosts*, designed by Irene Corey.

172. Left to right, (front) Sandra West as Maritorne, Charlie Brown as Sancho; (behind) Gary Ball as The Innkeeper, Allen Shaffer as Don Quixote in *Don Quixote of la Mancha*.

173. Paulette James as Major Barbara in Shaw's *Major Barbara*. Directed by Joe V. Graber at Centenary College, 1963.

174. Jimmy Journey as the hare, and Ken Holamon as the tortoise in *The Great Cross Country Race*.

INDEX

This index covers references in the text and illustrations: an illustration is noted by a page reference in *italic* type.

Biography

When Irene Corey is not designing specialty costumes and props for her company in Dallas, Texas, where she lives, she is planting ever more lilies and iris in her non-traditional garden. "Lawns are only useful if you play croquet." Neither the flowers, the bugs, or Flash, her striped cat, are free from the possibility of ending up as a color motif, or a makeup abstraction in one of her designs.

As a student of painting at Baylor University, she was lured into the theatre to "paint shadows on a set", and stayed to combine the two art forms into her own unique style of theatrical design. "I've always thought it strange to consider designing costumes for a headless body, so I design from top to toe." Her belief in thorough research and total design concept resulted in visual images which received recognition in world press and in leading publications concerning theatre. Her strength lies in her ability to unify through design, and perhaps in her ability to "look at one — and see another."

An extensive new look at her work for stage appears in the recent book *An Odyssey of Masquers: The Everyman Players*.

Photo by Suzanne Dietz